Cincinnati Ghosts
and Other
Tri-State Haunts

Karen
Laven

Schiffer
Publishing Ltd

4880 Lower Valley Road, Atglen, Pennsylvania 19310

Dedication

This book involved oodles of time, miles of travel, and limitless exploration (sometimes snowy, frigid, and muddy exploration); most of which my partner in life, and in this project, willingly gave. Doug, I've told you a hundred times; *I couldn't have done it without you.* I realize, however, that's probably not true. I *could* have done it without you, but it would have been missing *something special,* and it certainly wouldn't have been nearly as much fun.

Ouija® is a registered trademark of Parker Brother's Games

Schiffer Books are available at special discounts for bulk purchases for sales promotions or premiums. Special editions, including personalized covers, corporate imprints, and excerpts can be created in large quantities for special needs. For more information contact the publisher:

Published by Schiffer Publishing Ltd.
4880 Lower Valley Road
Atglen, PA 19310
Phone: (610) 593-1777; Fax: (610) 593-2002
E-mail: Info@schifferbooks.com

For the largest selection of fine reference books on this and related subjects,
please visit our web site at **www.schifferbooks.com**
We are always looking for people to write books on new and related subjects. If you have
an idea for a book please contact us at the above address.

This book may be purchased from the publisher.
Include $5.00 for shipping.
Please try your bookstore first.
You may write for a free catalog.

In Europe, Schiffer books are distributed by
Bushwood Books
6 Marksbury Ave.
Kew Gardens
Surrey TW9 4JF England
Phone: 44 (0) 20 8392-8585; Fax: 44 (0) 20 8392-9876
E-mail: info@bushwoodbooks.co.uk
Website: www.bushwoodbooks.co.uk

Designed by Mark David Bowyer
Type set in Burton's Nightmare 2000 / NewBskvll BT

ISBN: 978-0-7643-2899-2
Printed in the United States of America

Contents

Acknowledgments
Thank You...

Most every book I've ever read contains a thank you section; an area dedicated to several individuals and/or seemingly unending lists of people (most often people that I, the reader, have never heard of). I often wondered what the heck those "thanked" people did to wind up there. Now I know. When undertaking a book of this magnitude, you are plunked before the mercy of your fellowman, woman (and ghost!). It is up to them to decide *IF* they will talk with you.

Believe me, this isn't always as easy at it sounds. Multiple emails, phone calls, and personal approaches by this author went unheeded. It's as if I were as invisible as the subject I am writing about. Thankfully, there were many more who not only responded to my approaches, but also did so with modesty, honesty, humor, and warmth. I've met a wide conglomeration of wonderful human beings while researching this book on Tri-State ghosts, and it's been an honest privilege. Thank you to **all of you** who helped me navigate the ghost writing path; whether it was by telling your own tale, relaying someone else's accounts, and/or taking the time and effort to refer the author to pertinent sources. I appreciate each and every one of you.

Thank you, also, to Dinah Roseberry, my Schiffer editor, for giving me the opportunity to work with you. It's been an honor and a pleasure; you are as ingratiating as you are knowledgeable. Thank you, too, to my fellow Schiffer author, Sherry Strub, for always being there over the years, writing-wise and otherwise.

Thanks to Mike Palmer of Paranormal Investigations of Northern Kentucky for moving up that Middletown investigation so this author could come along for the ride. (Moreover, what a ride it was!) Thanks, also, to Brad Rubin of Paranormal Worlds for sharing his knowledge, advice and contacts with me. A huge thanks to Dennis Dalton (and the hospitality of Pam and Vickie at Angel of the Garden) for giving this author a version of your "Not So Dearly Departed Tour" of Waynesville and sharing your incredible knowledge along the way. A special thanks to Marlene Trapp for finagling interviews and other important information for the book.

Thanks, also, to Donna Clifton of Bobby Mackey's for tirelessly answering questions and allowing the author multiple visits. Thanks to Ronna Kaye Roe-Howard, for submitted photos and great contact information. Lisa Kinder-Cross and Jeff Kinder: thank you for the submitted photos. Thanks, also, to Andy Crosier and Shane Reinert of Dark Figure Productions; and to Richard Crawford, as well. Thanks go out to Jeremy Parnell; your referrals were terrific! Thanks to the *Ledger Independent Newspaper* in Maysville and to ALL the citizens of that town who shared their personal accounts and knowledge with me. Thanks for the tour, Anne and Keith Henderson! Thanks Sean (McHugh) for sharing your artistic talents (and your vision of Loretta) with all of us! Thanks goes out, as well, to the fine folks at the Alverta Green Museum in Mason, Ohio.

Thanks to my extended family for encouraging me to write all these years and, finally, thanks to my husband, Doug and our two boys, Jake and Luke, for doing without a fairly hefty portion of "Wife and/or Mom" time during this ghost writing process. You know I love you, and yeah, I know, I owe you.

Foreword

I was brought up to understand that an integral part of life is, ironically, death. After all, it is a huge perspective helper. We all know it's coming and we all know people who have passed on before us. We might not think about death all that much, but it's there alright; tucked beneath that *inevitable* sign stuck in the soil of our souls. We can't help but wonder what happens once the inevitability hits the fan and it's our turn.

Most of us are fairly certain in where we think we're headed—or hope to be, anyway—while others firmly believe that the buck stops here once our earthly vessel is kaput. Having witnessed some spiritual and profound (at least for me) incidents throughout my life, I have grown up grasping (pretty much right out of the gate) that there are things around me that I don't quite completely understand, and that's okay. Death is one of those things. Ghosts are another.

Just because I don't have a lock on the latter certainly doesn't mean they are not there. That's ludicrous. I staunchly believe they are here, hanging out, for whatever reason each one might have for doing so. I wrote about a particular paranormal experience following my father's death, and it was published in *FATE* Magazine years ago. The point being; long before I began this book, I *knew* they were there.

Interviewing people and visiting purported Tri-State haunted sites for this project, however, was further affirmation of how incredible the connections/effects between human beings and those who are visiting from another realm can truly be. During the six-month research and writing period of this book, I, personally, captured EVPs, and on more than several occasions had some rather inexplicable things happen at our family house that caused my husband to say: "Karen, quit bringing your work home with you!" He was serious. I heard many, many accounts, from across our cities and towns, too many to be able to share them all with you, but suffice it to say, that it was a relief for a good majority to share their tale, precisely because they truly seemed to believe with their whole being that what happened to them was real.

What follows are those accounts, sprinkled with some interesting history of our part of the country, with an urban legend or two thrown in for good measure. I thank you, reader, for opting to come along for the ride.

—Karen Laven

Introduction
Hunting for Haunts in the Tri-State

While hunting for ghosts is not as popular as going to the movies—yet!—more people than ever are expressing an interest in dipping their toes into the paranormal realm. After all, who doesn't love a great ghost movie? Moreover, how intriguing would it be to bring it to the next level by visiting a potentially haunted local site in person? Thankfully, Cincinnati not only offers the best chili in the country; it also offers plenty of haunted places to explore. Actually the city in southeastern Ohio banked on the river of the same name has so much history packed inside its overflowing borders that it would be surprising if there weren't ample paranormal accounts and more coming in all the time. Cincinnati and the tri-state area is covered in this book; and if you're on the lookout for some ghostly sites and accounts that will chill your spine and curl your toes? Well, you've come to the right place.

As the name indicates the tri-state includes areas not only within one state, but three. Along with Cincinnati and its surrounding portions of southeastern Ohio, there is also the smaller tip of southwestern Indiana and a good portion of northern Kentucky. Cincinnati and areas all around are teaming with tales of paranormal accounts. There are multiple tales from the top of Kentucky and lower Ohio this time around.

This book covers the gamut; from taverns to cemeteries, with lots of expected (and unexpected) places in between. You can have a spot of tea and some killer scones at several local haunted teahouses or peruse antiques (and spirits) at others, and stop for an icy cocktail at one of (if not *THE*) most haunted nightclubs in

America. We'll stroll around a charming Ohio town that also happens to be filled with ghost-ridden structures and you might elect to spend the night at an inn that houses paranormal guests as well as their human counterparts. Or you might decide to take a drive down some of the more notorious stretches of roadway around; places where strange, faceless creatures have been seen, roadsides that hold legends, rumors, past tragedies, and what seems like real danger. Within these pages you will also meet some open and successful individuals who have shared their personal experiences with the paranormal within their private homes and lives.

After interviewing several ghost hunting groups from around the tri-state, it was discerned that paranormal occurrences occur in a myriad of ways. One can hear voices, sounds, and footsteps, or detect certain smells. Feelings and emotions can come seemingly out of nowhere and so can full-blown apparition sightings (although rarely). There are no shortage of hauntings or ghost-hunters around these parts, that's for sure!

Mike Palmer, founder of Paranormal Investigators of Northern Kentucky (PINK), a non-profit organization in the state of Kentucky, has always had an interest in seeking out what is not easily explained; and has been obsessed with finding the answers. His group has been growing strong since 2005.

Whether one is conducting a formal investigation or just visiting a site rumored to have otherworldly visitors, it helps to know what to look for. There are several "types" of hauntings, and the odds are that if you do, indeed, encounter some paranormal activity, it will be through an imprint/residual haunting. Those are much more commonly found. An imprint is when something is repeated at certain intervals: A ghost pacing every night at the same time, or even once a year or once every ten years, for example. It's like watching the same "I Love Lucy" episode repeatedly, only without Lucy.

An intelligent haunting is less likely to occur than an imprint haunting, but is still a real possibility, as this author can now personally attest to (as revealed later on in the "What are these? EVPs?" chapter of this book). Intelligent hauntings can actually interact with individuals and their actions are geared to gaining people's attention and, sometimes, can annoy them to exasperation; much like a toddler's antics.

Another entity that is less commonly encountered on a ghost hunt is a poltergeist, which, by definition (German origin), means "noisy ghost." These are commonly believed to be unconsciously manifested by an individual in the home; usually a teenager approaching puberty.

Demonic entities are also a possibility; however, thankfully, they are very rare. Nevertheless, if there ever was a great reason for attempting to nurture a positive outlook—it's definitely when you are entering the ghost hunting venue. Negativity begets negativity.

Portal hauntings concern a specific area that is considered a doorway for the entities to pass through. Certain sites, such as Indian Burial Grounds, are believed to have a portal (doorway to another dimension) but they can be found pretty much anywhere (such as in the basement of Mackey's or the Westwood Town Hall in Cincinnati).

A ghost can look like a full-sized person, completely dressed and gallivanting around a structure or grounds (quite a rare sight) or it can be seen as a shadow, or maybe a wispy, filmy thing, like a fog or mist. It can also be invisible (much more commonplace).

Why do ghosts exist? Why are they still here? Sometimes it's reasoned that the "being" has unfinished business holding them to this plane. Perhaps it is a yearning to remain "home," at a familiar, beloved place. Alternatively, it could be something that could involve the being seeking some sort of justice or, even more unnerving—attempting to enact a form of revenge.

Some believe that there are those who've done malicious or harmful acts/deeds while of human flesh and body, and have stubbornly and successfully avoided continuing onward and upward (or is it downward?) in their spiritual journey following the death of their physical form. The thought of purgatory or hell waiting around the next bend is enough to keep them staunchly grounded on the earthly plane. I cannot imagine it's much fun, hanging around under such foreboding circumstances (and, hopefully, I'll never have to witness such a thing).

Palmer's "dream" as a tri-state ghost hunter is one that many ghost hunting individuals share: "To come face-to-face with something (paranormal) and being able to prove it," he says. A typical ghost hunting investigation begins with what might seem like mundane, but necessary tasks.

"The first thing we like to do, if possible, is research the property and try to find any events that took place in the past that might help explain what people are experiencing," notes Palmer. "We also interview anyone who has witnessed anything. Based on what we are told, we will try to one-by-one, find a real-world explanation."

Truth-be-told, it is vital for any ghost hunter to diligently strive to debunk a haunting. This not only helps to ensure competency and forthrightness, but also works to build a solid and reputable reputation in the ghost hunting business.

After the research is done, Palmer's group gets into action. "We then pick a day for the investigation, set up our equipment, and begin the investigation," he notes. "However, that is really just the beginning. There is much work still to be done.

"In the days following an investigation, we pour over hours of video and audio tape. We try to draw correlations from our instruments and weather/solar/atmospheric conditions. When we have been through everything, we present our findings to the client."

Brad Rubin, founder of Paranormalworlds.com, a paranormal investigation and informational web site, says that "Greater Cincinnati, generally speaking, seems to be a town with a lot of potential for uncovering paranormal activity. It's a major U.S. city that doesn't seem to have a lot of paranormal enthusiasts, or for that matter, people openly willing to let formal groups or experienced people investigate yet. Settlements here date back to the 1700s, and the history is immense, especially the historical towns along the river. So I would say Cincinnati has vast potential."

Being beckoned by worried home and business owners to help them out can be a true thrill. However, being on a case and seeing/feeling something strange and/or eerie can be something to reckon with on a personal level.

"I wouldn't say I've been afraid," says Palmer. "I mean, sure, the hair on my arms have stood up a few times, but I've never been fearful to go into a room, house, or tunnel." Palmer goes on to say that he has had certain team members who have been affected differently.

"[Some team members have] had bouts of fear," he notes. "Most recently, one team member became as he described as 'being washed over with raw emotion,'" says Palmer. "It took a lot out of him, and to this day, he really doesn't like to talk about it."

Palmer offers some advice for those who want to venture out their tri-state doors and do some ghost hunting themselves. "The best tip I can give is to get permission from the property owners. Don't just show up and start poking around; that's a good way to get arrested. Also during October, check the newspaper for events. Sometimes groups offer drive-by tours of haunted spots. There are some public places you can go that are likely to be haunted; such as the Loveland Castle. Check the Internet," Palmer says, adding that there are some ghost hunting groups that periodically offer a ghost hunting experience; albeit, for a fee. Most times, fees are used for equipment and other things that allow these groups to stay nonprofit and offer their services for free.

"Public investigations typically are large group outings where capturing solid evidence is nearly impossible usually," says Rubin. "Most paranormal activity is very subtle, but it is definitely there, if a place is truly active. You will be surprised at what you find on your audio and video when you review it later."

Palmer shares that the best evidence that PINK has come away with are EVPs, and he admits that even those "are few and far between." When it comes to ghost hunting, patience is not only a virtue, it's a necessity.

As for the orb debate, Palmer says that he believes orbs are "dust, moisture, or an out-of-focus insect. Orbs seem to appear everywhere." He adds that he knows that there are others who believe orbs could signal, at times, something paranormal, and that he respects their opinions.

Palmer counts Bobby Mackey's Music World (also featured in this book) as one of the most haunted tri-state sites and lists several area private homes as well. Rubin agrees that Mackey's is likely a haunted site, although he questions just how haunted it might be.

Sean Feeney, Director of the Anomaly Response Network, http://www.anomalyresponse.org) is a local, young ghost hunter that is doing what he is meant to do. Feeney says his group has been operating since the fall of 2001 as the Northern Kentucky Paranormal Youth Group (NKPYG). "My lifelong interest in the paranormal led me to join the Kentucky Mutual UFO Network (KYMUFON) in 2000," he says. However, Feeney was frustrated "at the denial of the value of the youth participation in paranormal investigations."

Feeney's group has been on cable specials (locally) since 2001 and has investigated major sites like Mackey's. Like Palmer and Rubin, Feeney will continue building his enterprise, investigating sites and striving to find the ultimate proof that the paranormal is as real as mom's apple pie…only not quite as tasty.

While visiting some of the haunted sites listed in this book remember; get permission and don't trespass, no matter how tempting the thought might be. Once you're cleared to take a legal look, keep in mind that you don't need special, expensive equipment, or even a course in Ghost Hunting 101. All you need to do is bring along what the good Lord gave you: your sense of touch, smell, taste, hearing, sight, and intuition. Reports of paranormal behavior almost always stem from someone just like you; cooking, working around the house, visiting a local tavern, just living life. Most didn't go looking for a ghostly encounter; it just came to them. Trust your gut, open your mind, and above all, have a great time!

Chapter 1
Hayswood Hospital in Maysville

Hayswood Hospital in Maysville, Kentucky, once a thriving medical facility is now a rusty, tattered shell. This decaying structure sitting atop a hill on 4th Street in Maysville overlooking the grand Ohio River and the Simon Kenton Bridge is a prime example of what happens when a building is left to survive of its own accord since 1983.

Mother Nature, vandals, and neglect pick it apart until the once-gleaming structure becomes just about as hazardous to one's health as it is possible to be. Floors, littered with fallen insulation and debris, can break through without warning, filth (and, likely vermin) runs rampant, and there is something in the air in addition to mold and asbestos—the gut feeling that this three-story structure is also harboring unsettled spirits from beyond.

Hayswood Hospital in Maysville, Kentucky, has been abandoned (by humans, at least) since 1983.

This is likely what beckons some to ignore the "No Trespassing" signs (and the very real chance of being arrested) and enter a once pristine and medicinal confine. In its heyday, it was where individuals from a six-county area went for treatment of a variety of ailments, from commonplace maladies to life-threatening emergencies. Babies were born there, lives were saved there, people died there. The glory days long gone now, it is a decaying corpse of abandonment. Its windows are broken, leafy tree branches creep through the curtains into the empty rooms. Clocks still hang on the walls, trays and lockers are scattered about; gurneys stand in the hall waiting for patients that will never again be admitted.

Truth be told, it looks as if the building was left quickly and suddenly, because a complete exodus was never carried out. Even decades later, some equipment and supplies remain. Perhaps that's why some of the ghostly residents have never left.

Hayswood Seminary (built in the 1800s) was the first building on that site. Then May Peale Wilson came on the scene and turned it into the Wilson Infirmary, which ran until she died in 1908. It was 1915 when the first bricks were laid for the Hayswood Hospital that stands today (along with additions in 1925 and 1971). The eighty-seven-bed facility bit the figurative dust in 1983 in conjunction with the unveiling of the Meadowview Regional Medical Center.

Going up? Wheelchair access and the morgue entrance were both located on the front lower portion of the hospital grounds.

The town of Maysville hasn't decided whether it is wiser to refurbish the structure into an apartment building or tear it down for additional parking space. Some people believe that it could be a wonderful tourist draw for ghost hunting groups. Several have already gone through the site and more would likely come if it were made available, including nationally known groups. Others don't want that particular aspect expounded upon and fear that the building has eroded into something far too dangerous to tread within.

Since its closing, rumors about it being haunted have run as rampant as the vines growing outside (and inside) the hospitals façade: Reports of babies crying, visions of phantom doctors roaming the halls, a woman staring out of the upstairs window, gurneys moving, seemingly at will, and lots of ghostly footsteps and voices are heard.

Keith Henderson of Maysville claims the hospital was haunted long before it was abandoned. When he had been hospitalized after an accident, he recalls waking up to see two nurses in his room that he knew did not work there. He mumbled something to them and suddenly, they were gone. "I knew everybody that worked there," says Henderson, "and I'd never seen them before."

The courtyard at Hayswood Hospital has seen better days. Check out the section below (left of) the basketball hoop; it has a strange, smudged appearance. *Photo courtesy of Jeff Kinder & Lisa Kinder-Cross.*

Ronna Kaye Roe-Howard, a ghost hunter from Maysville, visited Hayswood Hospital with the investigative ghost hunting group, East Side Paranormal Society (founders are Vince and Tammy Hardy), in 2007, but it was not the first time she'd been in the structure by any means.

"I was a nurse there many years ago," writes Roe-Howard via email, "and know the rooms well. We have been to Hayswood Hospital on two occasions. We shot pictures from within what used to be the morgue. What we got is a huge white mist that covers a part of the area." Several other individuals have claimed to have strange things happen in that area of the hospital, as well, including shadows and the sounds of imminent footsteps.

"We took a picture from the outside, of a second floor window," notes Roe-Howard. "In the first shot, there is what looks like a huge piece of hospital equipment in the window area. We took another shot immediately and the object was no longer there."

Roe-Howard goes on to write that "a dear friend once went into the hospital when it was closed. On the second floor she reported seeing a shadow of a woman." Her friend shared that the shadow woman was "holding a baby and crying. She said the features of the woman were not clear, but she could recognize the baby if she saw it again. According to Roe-Howard's friend: "as fast as she appeared, she disappeared."

On another hospital excursion after its closing, this same friend and two others entered the hospital, again, after the electric and water had already been turned off. The trio was helping to remove some of the equipment from the site.

"They heard a noise," says Roe-Howard, and the small group immediately stopped what they were doing. "As they stood there, the elevator door opened, a gurney rolled out and down the hallway, and the elevator door closed again. Remember, there was no longer electric in the building," notes Roe-Howard.

Strange sights and sounds have been observed as far as the other side of the road from the abandoned structure. Roe-Howard shares that "people who live across the street from the hospital have seen the figure of a lady in a second floor window," and that "lights are reported to be on once in a while in various rooms."

Lisa Kinder-Cross grew up in Maysville but has lived in Lexington for the last quarter century. Her brother, Jeff Kinder, now lives in Orlando, Florida, but the duo has not forgotten their Maysville roots.

Lisa notes via email that it was in the summer of 2005 when he was up visiting, that she and her brother "decided our yearly adventure would be to take a 'tour' through Hayswood Hospital on a Sunday morning." Having grown up in town, the two were curious to see what the hospital now looked like inside after standing empty for so long.

"Since we remembered, somewhat, the layout of the hospital, we went behind the hospital, dropped down into the old patio area and entered the basement floor through there," shares Kinder-Cross.

It was a tour of a lifetime, to be sure. "Some of the hallways were so dark," Kinder-Cross writes, "that we had to use the flash on my camera to light

The view from the pediatric ward at Hayswood was a stunner, showcasing the Ohio River and the Simon Kenton Bridge. The brother and sister felt safest at that site. *Photo courtesy of Jeff Kinder & Lisa Kinder-Cross.*

our way—it was a spur of the moment decision so we didn't have flashlights!"

The pair also visited the abandoned pediatrics ward. "It felt safe and protected in that area," says Kinder-Cross, "and we both kind of dreaded having to go back through the hospital to get back outside."

"One specific room gave Jeff Kinder a very distinct feeling "that the patient in this room was abandoned when the hospital was shut down." He says he felt "like we were intruding on someone when we were in that room and we shouldn't be in there."

The duo continued through the hallways, checking out the rooms, hallways, and nurses stations, and ultimately made their way to the upper level.

"We found our way to the third floor and were going by a nurses' station (completely intact!) when we heard what sounded exactly like someone running in heels in the hallway coming up behind us. [We] ran into a room to hide since we did ignore the big "No Trespassing" sign out in front of the hospital," Kinder-Cross admits. "We thought we had been seen sneaking in and were being chased, until we looked down at the floor. The floors are wet with insulation that has fallen out of the ceilings over the years. There is no way to actually make that clacking sound! To compose ourselves and continue, we decided it must have been water dripping somewhere in the hospital. The clacking sound stopped as suddenly as it started and lasted approximately thirty seconds, so we continued our adventure."

After thinking it over, the brother and sister team realize that they could have gotten injured and/or in trouble with the law while visiting Hayswood. "We would never again trespass," says Kinder-Cross, "nor would we advise anyone else to—especially after we saw how structurally unsafe it was on the inside.

Michael Wheeler would agree.

Falling ceilings, standing water and sopping-wet insulation litter the once-immaculate halls of Hayswood Hospital.
Photo courtesy of Jeff Kinder & Lisa. Kinder-Cross.

"I have never seen [my brother] unnerved until inside that hospital that day!" Kinder-Cross shares. "Some of our photos were shot blindly down hallways of total darkness," she says, "and when I asked [my brother] if he had found anything after looking closer in his pics, he had noticed some of the exact things I had."

"In one hallway," Kinder-Cross continues, "I shot a picture of him getting ready to go into a room. At the very end of this hallway, there is a shadow figure in front of a door! I had never looked at the little details in these pics before, but the shadow is totally too wide to be him (the shadowy figure is also facing forward and Jeff Kinder is facing sideways). "It is not his shadow," says Kinder-Cross. "Hard to explain…"

Jeff Kinder plays "Vanna White" in Hayswood, showcasing the old stove, cabinet and fluorescent lights that appear lit—without benefit of electricity. *Photo courtesy of Jeff Kinder & Lisa Kinder-Cross.*

Wheeler has lived in Maysville for most of his life and his interest in Hayswood Hospital has spanned the majority of his years on this earth. Wheeler created the Hayswood Hospital Myspace.com group in order to "connect with others who have felt the, for lack of a better word, evil, that comes from the hospital," writes Wheeler via email.

"I used to go in often with friends as a kid, because it was the thing to do," Wheeler shares, "and we would always get freaked out. Now, sometimes I'll be honest, I think it was more because we wanted to be scared but there were times when strange things did happen." Wheeler recalls when he and his friends moved a stretcher. "We actually flipped it over," he writes, "and when we returned to the same hall, the stretcher was [back upright] where we'd first seen it. There was mud all over the floor (which is odd as well, why is there mud all over the place?) and I knew we left tracks and they were not there."

Jeff Kinder and his unknown "friend" at the end of the hall.
Photo courtesy of Jeff Kinder & Lisa Kinder-Cross.

Wheeler also shares that they also witnessed "eyes peering out of the kitchen/commons area which was pitch black." It could have been any given animal, but it freaked me out, though, 'cause you never know."

What Wheeler is sure about, however, is what he heard. "I did hear a heart monitor though, plain as anything," he shares. A heart monitor's beeping in a building with no electricity since 1983? Unnerving to be sure. "I could swear I heard voices, too," he adds.

Although Wheeler admits he's never seen any ghosts or shadows, he did "feel very cold in areas that shouldn't have been. This was back when I was a teenager before I even thought of watching all these haunting shows. What I felt was real," he says. "I don't believe in many things but when you feel a cold like that in the dead of summer, it stays with you. I've heard, and since read, many things about Hayswood; learning of adventures of others who dared enter, which I must warn is illegal. A friend of mine and I were arrested coming out of the hospital," he notes. "The cops assumed we had gone in to smoke weed, but we were charged with third degree trespassing and criminal mischief."

That was enough for Wheeler; he hasn't ventured back inside since, and he strongly urges others not to trespass as well. "I have just always wanted to prove that this place was really haunted," avers Wheeler, "if not to anyone but to myself. It's a scary place, even for me; there are rooms that chill you to the bone even in the mid-summer heat. Some areas are pitch black when there's no reason for them to be. We felt like we were being followed."

These are but a few of the countless stories of unexplained visions and sounds inside that decaying structure. Its future remains clouded in doubt as its past continues to roam the halls.

Hayswood Hospital is located on 4th Street in Maysville, Kentucky.

Chapter 2
Buffalo Ridge

Hamilton County, Ohio, has more than its share of ghostly inhabitants scattered about. One can traverse the county from top to bottom and side to side and hear numerous tales of visitors that are claimed to hail from the land of the unexplained. It has been said that Ohio is one of the most haunted states in the country and that just might be the case.

Buffalo Ridge is a long, windy, road that slowly chugs upward toward the heavens. It rests at the edge of Hamilton County, close to the border of Indiana. The narrow lane rambles by houses, fields, and the Mitchell Memorial Forest; a state park that offers plenty of natural fun. This road is really quite breathtaking, (for several, vastly different reasons) for, although the road is lined with beautiful trees, heights, and stunning hilltop views, it feels suffocating at times—as if the lush environment is slowly but surely closing in on you.

There are more than just a couple of stories/legends about the goings on around the road—especially at nighttime. Rumors abound, too numerous and varied to mention them all.

It has been said, for example, that Satanists have used the vast bowels of the wooded area to perform their satanic rites, and that the repercussions are vile. There was also a long standing rumor that a crematorium once conducted their business there.

The crematorium commotion has since been debunked, however. Local ghost hunter, twenty-one-year-old student from Fairfield, Ohio, Alex Scales, shares the real truth: The remains are that of a planetarium (now abandoned), which was the first planetarium for the city of Cincinnati.

An abandoned house along the road was the source for many sightings of strange lights and even the vision of a "witch" in one of the home's windows. The buildings have since been torn down, but a strange fog does remain at one site, even when other surrounding areas have no trace of the white stuff. It was seen and photographed by this author on a warm springtime afternoon.

Another tale from Buffalo Ridge concerns that of an "evil" dark, black van that is said to traverse the road periodically. The vehicle's windows are tinted and several people have said that this foreboding van has "chased" them while they were traveling along the scenic road.

Toss in a small dog with evil eyes, a dead, white-wearing bride, a vicious, snarling green-eyed, canine, and unfulfilled body part roundups by ghosts in search of their missing legs and arms and you've got lots to absorb when taking a drive up the ridge.

Scales shares that his high school English teacher admitted that he and a friend had driven out to Buffalo Ridge and that they were snooping around a barn there. They opened the door to peek inside and saw a bloodletting of chickens. The unfortunate fowl were chained from the ceiling, their bright red drops of blood plunking atop the old leaves beneath them. The teacher and his cohort quickly hightailed it outta there in their vehicle and were chased along by a huge truck until they were off the road entirely. Could just be an irate farmer but his teacher was not so sure. Who knows? There have also been numerous sightings of a white van chasing motorists out of the area, which Scales and some others chalk up to park rangers, not ghosts, since the rangers drive white vehicles.

Right:
An abandoned lot on Buffalo Ridge. Strange fog, lights and other anomalies have been seen here.

Given all the debunking Scales has done, it is interesting to note that the young adult did have an experience that he cannot explain away on Buffalo Ridge—an experience that contained none of the elements of the urban legend of this remarkable stretch of road, but all of the fear.

It began not too long ago when Scales graciously opted to give a tour of Buffalo Ridge to several friends who were unfamiliar with the area. The trio (Scales, his friend, and his friend's girlfriend) got to the ridge about nine pm. Once there, they strolled past the "No Dumping" sign and down the trail that leads to the area where the remnants of the Planetarium rest.

"Being the loser who loves to tell the local history that I am, I was talking pretty loudly about the area, while Kay and Jonathan walked behind me," wrote Scales of his encounter on the www. yourghoststory.com web site.

Scales noted that his friends held several flashlights so they would see where they were going, while Scales opted to wing his way through the darkness—up at the front, no less. He was, however, still able to lead them to the foundation of the Planetarium, which by then was reduced to "a bunch of bricks and torn metal in the hillside."

The group took a load off for about half an hour, chatting about mundane things and getting a feel for their surroundings. Suddenly, Kay noticed that there was something different in the way the air felt, which prompted Scales to jump down into the depths of the foundation and start scrounging around. Kay was already unnerved and quite ready to leave at this juncture, but Scales was on the other side of the site, searching for any clues. At this point, it was noted that Jonathan agreed it was time to skedaddle out of there, so Scales began making his way out.

When interviewed about his experience, Scales expounded: "I shined my light back up the wall I had climbed down to see Kay and Jonathan, when I saw [a man]," notes Scales. "I didn't get a good look at the man, but he appeared to be wearing black clothes and walking fairly swiftly through the foliage."

"I personally recall seeing a figure moving past some trees above me while I heard sticks breaking and leaves rustling, and I could have sworn I saw a pale face with glasses," Scales adds. "Honestly, I figured it was a local homeowner coming to tell us to get lost! Later, I found that my friends had seen the same figure I had, and they described him as an 'old farmer.'"

"Eventually I made it up the wall," says Scales, "and no one was *freaken* there!" Not even his friends; and certainly not the man he'd seen just a few minutes ago. "Annoyed, I walked back up the trail to Buffalo Ridge, and found Kay crying while Jonathan hugged her," he continues. "So, I asked what happened to our guest, when Jonathan starts raging on and on about how 'this dude just totally came out of nowhere, walked right up to me….and vanished!'"

Talk about hitting ghost hunting pay dirt. The two young adult males were exceedingly thrilled, while Kay, on the other hand, was exceedingly frightened. Scales admitted that he was upset that he didn't get to see "a ghost walk up to me and disappear."

When asked to further describe the experience, Scales says that it was simply awesome. "I was pretty excited, but also jealous since I didn't witness him disappearing. Part of me still wonders if we might have (somehow all imagined) the experience, but I have trouble believing that."

Buffalo Ridge is located in Cleves, Ohio. To get there from Cincinnati, take I-74 to Cleves exit, right on Route 128 to Miami town, right on Harrison Avenue, right on East River Road, left on Gum Rum Road, right on Buffalo Ridge Road.

Chapter 3
Chateau LaRouch

"**I** know they know you're coming," Sir Joe remarks to this visiting author at the Historic Loveland Castle Museum in Loveland, Ohio. "They hear," he adds with a sly grin. "They are upset about some of the people that come out here that they don't like. You can just tell. They play games."

Sir Joe is one of the Loveland Castle Knights of the Golden Trail (the name of the area's Boy Scout Troop). He's been at the castle since the early 1960s. The knights inherited the castle from Sir Harry Andrews, the castle's mastermind and creator, after Sir Harry's death.

Loveland Castle is an incredible testament to Sir Harry Andrews, and his remarkable vision. It's a showcase for what the act of perseverance and diligence can achieve. It might also, perhaps, be a place for his spirit to perpetually hang out, and the spirits of several others as well. One thing's for certain: There are definitely some strange things going on there.

Sir Harry decided to build the castle alongside a river and the woods knowing it would be a perfect place for area Boy Scout troops to meet and hold their activities. Granted, by the time he was finished, the "boys" in the initial troop were bringing their grandsons to the site.

Sir Joe points to a table with a conglomeration of playing pieces on top. "You wanna play a game?" he says. "We'll play a game." Sir Joe says that if you set the pieces up before bed, when you get up in the morning they will be moved around. Game playing with ghosts? Talk about coming to the right place.

Imagine not only having a rousing tabletop showdown with the otherworld, but also spending the night inside a real castle; with the otherworld as slumber party guests. It's possible to do both at this incredible medieval-looking structure. The castle welcomes visitors (for a small fee) to tour the castle (hours and days vary according to season) and take in all that the museum has to offer—including ghosts.

The castle ghosts are not only fun loving but are rather invaluable to the success of the place. They take it upon themselves to alert the knights to misdeeds taking place on the grounds and they have even thwarted the efforts of a group of thieves attempting to break in; several times. Sounds too incredible to be real, doesn't it? Well, it *is* incredible, and it *is* real.

That is just part of the paranormal action that takes place pretty much daily in the brick fortress that juts upwards beside the banks of the flowing Little Miami River in Loveland, Ohio.

Sir Harry began construction of Loveland Castle (also known as Chateau LaRouch) in 1929. Over the next fifty years, he continued to build the one-fifth scale replicate of a tenth century Norman castle, one homemade stone at a time. He was an innovative fellow—a road scholar with a genius IQ—and his ingenuity was evident in the castle structure itself. When building the castle, he used empty milk cartons as cement-block molds. In order to make them lighter and easier to work with, he stuck an empty pop can in the center. Harry recycled before it was even a word, Sir Joe shares. He was innovative to say the least.

The castle has many rooms, all of them unique. There is the dungeon, a ballroom, a chapel, gardens, towers, and an undeniable sense of history and European flair. The front door is studded with 2, 530 nails and over three layers of wood. This, according to Sir Harry, "in order to prevent anyone from chopping through with an ax."

Inside the castle, are treasured items including a suit of armor, Coat of Arms, throne, and other artifacts from around the globe. There is a room devoted to continuously playing videos about Sir Harry and his castle construction.

Chateau LaRouch, also known as Loveland Castle was designed and built by Sir Harry Andrews (brick-by-brick) over a span of forty years. It's haunted, of course.

Sir Harry was ninety one years old when he died in 1981, and he was still active and productive. He certainly wasn't senile, notes Sir Joe. Sir Harry used to burn his trash, and on that one dire occasion, the polyester pants he was wearing caught on fire. Gangrene set in and he died of infection. His ashes are scattered outside the castle.

Sir Harry was destined to live an incredible life from the get-go. For one thing, he had been declared "dead" long before he built the castle. He was pronounced a goner at Fort Dix of spiral meningitis or encephalitis. He literally lay in the morgue for two days, and it was only discovered that he was alive when they started the autopsy and Sir Harry started bleeding.

"Dead men don't bleed," says Sir Joe. "Your heart has to pump for that." The coroner put adrenaline in Sir Harry's heart to kick-start it and he was saved. He then was sent to Europe where he worked as a medic in the service. His girlfriend left him and married somebody else while he was there and he never got over that, says Sir Joe.

To top it off, the modern way of warfare didn't sit well with him. He didn't believe it was moral. If battling had to be done, Sir Harry felt it should be done hand-to-hand, such as with swords. The medic saw many corpses of his fellow serviceman and it was especially hard for him to sign the death certificates of men who didn't die in battle. Sir Harry believed that they were all heroic. "I hope that he'll be inducted into the Veteran's Hall of Fame," notes Sir Joe.

Even before his death, there were some strange happenings at the Chateau. "Sir Harry used to write it in our *Golden Grail* paper that he would see an image that would knock on his door," says Sir Joe. "He would ask him to come in and [the spirit] would never come in. It was a knight from the past that would come up to talk to him. Sir Harry said it looked like a Norman knight, and I've seen the same thing over the years, but some [of the other Knights/visitors] see a lady."

Sir Joe went on to share that Boy Scouts stay overnight often, "and sometimes you'll have a kid take something." When this happens, shoes might be found hanging somewhere tied by the laces, alerting Sir Joe that something was awry. He confidently states that there is always some clue left by the ghost(s) if a kid has taken something, and when queried about it, the kids are often shocked (comically so) that they've somehow been found out.

In addition, items set down in one place can be missing only to be discovered in another part of the castle. "Oh, yeah, the ghosts can move things," Sir Joe shares.

You'll notice that Sir Joe says ghosts, as in plural. "There can be quite a few ghosts (at one time)," he admits. "I don't know if they're holding meetings here or if their cousins are coming or if this is their heaven here or what."

Sir Joe looks upon the spirits in the castle as "our guardians that guard the castle. I actually think there were two kids that died in a fire back in the old days (the twenties or the thirties) and all the things that go on here—schools, scouts, weddings birthday parties, they get to be here for. We've had ghost hunters come out and they say something is there but they don't know what—they can't figure it out," he adds.

Sir Joe guesstimates that the boy spirit that inhabits the castle is about thirteen and that the girl is closer to age seven. He added that a paranormal investigative group came out with an infrared camera and says there was a short one and a taller one. "Harry had said there was a fire up here and kids were killed, so it fits," Sir Joe adds.

There are so many instances of unexplained phenomena that the knights are actually quite accustomed to it, and, indeed, welcoming of it. "It's an ongoing thing," says Sir Joe, but he does admit that it took him a while to get used to it.

"I was here with my daughter right after Sir Harry died and we were getting ready to leave, and the door closed and locked," Sir Joe says. "All my hair was standing up everywhere—standing straight up."

"Are you all right?" he was asked.

"Yeah," he replied. "But I think I just got tickled. My daughter [looked at me] and started crying and said, 'Daddy, you've been tickled by a ghost!'"

The ghosts at Loveland Castle are not only pranksters and detectives, they also serve to keep things running smoothly at the site. "They'll tell us when the septic tank is getting full," Sir Joe says. "They let us know by slamming the door to the bathroom."

While he was still alive, Sir Harry slept down in the office of the castle, on a cot. "After he died, if you put anything on that cot, it would be on the floor. We set t-shirts on the cot one night and the next morning we found them on the floor. He didn't want anything set on his cot. We got the message to leave his cot alone!"

Sir Harry seemed to know all along that there were some otherworldly visitors that enjoyed his castle as much as their human counterparts.

"I think the [ghost] kids were here before Harry died because all these things were going on while he was alive," says Sir Joe. He admits that listening to those stories Sir Harry would tell could be challenging sometimes.

"You would think he was an eccentric old man telling ghost stories. We thought, "He's telling us that so we'll stay out of his stuff…" Sir Joe laughs. "Come to find out later that it was all true!"

Sir Joe knows that turnabout is fair play. Over and over, the ghost stories would be told and inside he was thinking: "Do you think I believe this?" Sir Joe tosses his arms in the air. "And later on, you're telling the same story and getting the same reaction."

The knights of Loveland Castle are not the only individuals who've seen, felt, or heard strange things at the medieval site.

"People send pictures with ectoplasm showing in it. I think they're just angels," says Sir Joe. "I don't believe in ghosts, I believe in angels."

Everyone seems to have their own idea of exactly what or who is hanging around the castle, but whatever you want to call them, the results are the same. Doors close and lock on their own, voices are heard, footsteps echo on the stairs, all hailing from no human source, etc.

What a perfect spot for young men to explore: year after year, night after night, local scouting troops get the chance to sleepover at the castle—and live to tell about it!

"Look at the thousands of kids that stay all night; they get up in the morning, leave here this much taller," says Sir Joe, his hand raised over his head. "They got to stay overnight in a haunted castle and they didn't get ate up or chewed up! They made it!" he chuckles. "The longer the kids stay up and tell ghost stories, the more things happen. They [the spirits/angels] are right there with you, having just as much fun."

The castle spirits are always on guard even when the knights are asleep. "If there's somebody snooping outside the [ghosts] will bang on the door so loud to wake me up and let me know that somebody is climbing outside and might get hurt," says Sir Joe. "I've had so many ear operations and I don't hear real good and [the angels make sure to bang loud enough to wake me up]." Sir Joe was able to locate the area where the thieves were coming in.

"Before that, the thieves had stolen Sir Harry's World War I medals and we didn't know how it was happening," says Sir Joe, "and if it hadn't been for the guardians we'd never know. They concentrate on one spot until we figure it out." He credits the ghosts for the capture of the thieves.

One thing Sir Joe is sure about is that the spirits have been around a long, long time. "They were here before me, now that Harry's gone, you gotta figure all this stuff out. There are things he told us that we should have paid more attention to!" He laughs and adds, "These are angels, have no fear, but I do think they mess with you if you're afraid, though. There's stuff happening almost daily—especially if you're here by yourself." Other employees and visitors report hearing/seeing things all the time.

According to Sir Joe, it is the castle tower that is the most haunted. "There's just something about getting your picture taken around that tall tower," he says. "Several people have sent us photos of the tower surrounded by a mist substance that was not visible when the photo was snapped."

Sir Joe has become extremely appreciative of the spirits/angels in the castle. After all, they have helped him out on numerous occasions.

"They are guardians—they are taking care of the place. If something needs to be done that you ain't done, they're gonna let you know about it."

Sir Joe believes that these original angels/spirits in the castle act as a sort of welcoming committee for other ghosts/angels that might be around.

"They must draw/lure [the other ghosts] here because the ones that people see outside are different. They see mist/ectoplasm. The children [spirits] mostly stay inside," says Sir Joe.

Loveland Castle has been a frequent stop for psychics and other paranormal groups over the years. Sir Joe recalls the time in 1983 when a local psychic came out to try and help them find a secret room. "I asked her if we could tape the conversation," says Sir Joe. "We went downstairs [to the dungeon area] and all of the sudden [she fell ill and dropped to the floor] and I thought she was dying. There was another lady and her son here and her husband. I carried her upstairs and her husband started swinging at me (thinking I was up to no good with his wife!)," says Sir Joe, laughing at the memory. "When I listened to that tape though," he adds with seriousness, "Names and dates came right over the tape—it was the voice of Sir Harry. That was a trip. I heard his voice again, plain as day. That's when the psychic started moaning and groaning and fell. The last thing Harry said on the tape was, "eat no pork.'"

So…does Sir Joe dare to eat pork after that dire warning?

"Yeah," he says with a shrug and a grin. Sir Joe takes everything in stride; even warnings from beyond.

"It doesn't faze me," he says. "I talk about it because there's no fear." He admits, however, that not everyone feels the same way when it comes to the castle. "My wife will not stay here. She is scared to death. When I tell her this stuff she says: 'You're an idiot!'" Sir Joe chuckles. "I say to her, 'have you ever seen me hurt or scared or something like that?' She admits that no, she hasn't. But she still won't stay."

The dungeon of Loveland Castle (seen here) is where Sir Joe's tape recorder picked up Sir Harry's voice—years after Sir Harry had died.

Right:
Knights, Coats of Armor and irreplaceable artifacts are housed within the Chateau LaRouch in Loveland, Ohio.

The castle is open for tours and can be booked for overnight stays. It has a seventy-plus year history with the local Boy Scouts, however, and that is its main mission. "Friday nights are theirs," says Sir Joe. "If people want to stay overnight in midweek, we can talk [for a fee]. Kids first."

People book the castle for ghost hunts, parties or weddings— there is a chapel in the castle as well as outside by the river. "Lots of them dress up in medieval garb for the weddings," says Sir Joe.

Come what may, whatever games they want to play, you can bet Sir Joe is staying put at the castle—ghosts/angels and all. Why would he ever want to leave? "It's too much fun," he says.

The address for the Historic Loveland Castle Museum is P.O. 135 in Loveland, Ohio 45140. The Web site is www.lovelandcastle.com.

The brick archway feels ultra-European and sublimely spooky!

Chapter 4
Crisis Center
Counselors from Beyond

T here is a building in Kentucky that is a respite for women who are in need of help due to domestic violence and/or sexual assault. It is an older building that has served several purposes. For example, it was a bicycle shop, a doctor's office, and an optometrist's office. It's most notorious (and boisterous) life, however, was that of a nineteenth century tavern. In its bar days for some of the more amorous bar patrons, there were sleeping quarters upstairs that came complete with a variety of painted ladies occupying them, says Beverly* an employee at the Crisis Center. It appears that one of those ladies of the evening has stayed put in the building, and the current occupants have taken to calling their resident female ghost *Miss Kitty*. Seems *Miss Kitty* is not wanting for company, as the sounds of a male from beyond have been detected in the building as well.

In more recent years, the upper floor of the building was used as a shelter for the women and children, but about three years ago, the shelter portion was moved off site. At that time strange things began happening with much greater frequency.

Prior to that, files might go missing or footsteps might periodically be noticed, but it wasn't excessive by any means. When renovation efforts were put into place for the upper space, however, the spirits really hit the fan, so to speak.

"Since the renovations, we can differentiate between an inside call and an outside call in this building," says Beverly. "All of the employees can be sitting around this table and be eating lunch and someone's phone will ring as an inside call." How is that possible? They have no clue. Perhaps *Miss Kitty*'s making prank calls?

"We hear people [meaning those who are not human] talking all the time," says Beverly. "I was in my office, all by myself, and I could hear a man and a woman arguing. I went and looked out front and out back and there was nobody there. As soon as I opened the door to go upstairs, the voices stopped. I couldn't tell what they were talking about, but it was two distinct voices, a male and a female."

Recently, two of the employees heard a male voice in the building even though there were no males around. "It sounded like it was coming from upstairs," says the employee. "I also heard a female voice yesterday, and it was muffled; you know, I can't make out what she said, and if you say something to it, it doesn't respond and the voice stops."

They work at lot on weekends, says Beverly, and their director does, as well. "The last two weeks we've both been in the building by ourselves at different times," she shares. "I was in the building alone and heard the bell on the second entrance door ring, indicating someone had come in. The front door was locked and no one could have gotten in from off the street, and there was just one of us in the building." There goes *Miss Kitty* again…

The director, Jamie*, tended to pooh-pooh the claims of the employees; that is, until she experienced them firsthand. Jamie was working alone on a weekend and she heard the bell ring on the door. Of course, she figured it was Beverly coming to work. Jamie waited and Beverly didn't appear, so she got up and checked and found nobody there. Then she went back to her desk and her phone rang. It was an internal call. Given the fact that she was the only person in the building, this was a bit of a shocker. The director picked up the phone and heard nothing, only to hang it up and have it ring again. After the sixth time her internal phone rang, she had had enough and said out loud: "*Miss Kitty*, leave me the hell alone!"

Miss Kitty complied, says Beverly with a laugh since Jamie received no more internal calls from beyond that day. Just to be sure it wasn't a phone malfunction, the group called out the phone expert who checked the system and found nothing awry.

It's not just phone calls and bell ringing that goes on, either. The employees also hear furniture moving upstairs. In addition, *Miss Kitty* has enjoyed locking them out of the building. Brisk footsteps are commonplace; they hear her footsteps up and down the halls, and files and reports go missing, courtesy of their resident ghost, only to reappear precisely where they initially left them.

"[The paranormal activity] has not died down," says Beverly, even though the renovation is now completed, a fact that surprises them. They have converted the upstairs into two apartments and can hardly wait to see what happens once the new tenants move in.

"I don't feel threatened or anything," says Beverly. "Sometimes it's real cold and sometimes I feel like people are watching me, but I'm not scared."

Miss Kitty is more a prankster than anything as evidenced by her most recent stunt: "I carried twenty-five chairs up those steps one time (leaving the door open)," Beverly comments, "and every time I'd get back up to the top of the stairs, the door would be shut," she adds with an exasperated sigh.

One night, they thought someone had broken in, but found out nobody had. They went over the tapes from the security camera and saw a woman. That doesn't sound so unusual until you hear from Beverly that the "woman was hovering atop the upper part of the outside of the building."

Beverly and the other employees have talked about having some area ghost hunters out to investigate their building one day, but only out of curiosity. Truth is, they are fine co-existing with the fun-loving painted lady and her gentleman ghost in their midst. In a place where they are there to guide their fellow women through difficult and/or sorrowful times, it helps to have someone fun-loving around like *Miss Kitty*.

---

* *Names changed for anonymity purposes.*

Chapter 5
The Faceless Hitchhiker of Dead Man's Curve

*Be careful of the path you choose, for you
never know where some roads might take you…*

Many towns across the U.S. have a road that is notoriously difficult to navigate. Sometimes the situation is exacerbated by inclement weather or by poor driving skills. Sometimes bad things happen for no explainable reason on a road that elicits a resounding sense of dread. Sometimes a shadow figure, a faceless shadowy figure, is seen hovering around the ditch by a wide range of people, slipping in and out of view. Sometimes it's all of the above: Dead Man's Curve between the towns of Amelia and Bethel in Clermont County, Ohio, is one of those roads.

This scary stretch of pavement runs through the village of Bantam, Ohio, where State Route 125 and 222 meet. It lies seemingly benign and in wait for its next victim. It doesn't appear deadly; it doesn't appear ominous. Perhaps that's how it's been able to lure so many down its perilous path. It's fairly widely known around these parts that anyone who dares to travel east of the Starlight Drive-In between the towns of Amelia and Bethel—especially between the hours of 1:20 to 1:40 **in the dead of morning** is taking a chance with fate.

Out of the starting gate, this road meant trouble. Dead Man's Curve was part of the Ohio Turnpike, a two-lane roadway that was originally built in 1831. The initial road was ridiculously designed in that it curved sharply right atop a steep hill. No wonder it was commonplace for individuals to take the curve too quickly and end up slipping over and rolling to their death below the hillside.

Officials recognized that it was a hazard from the get-go and, finally, in 1968, it was straightened out and expanded into a four-lane highway. There was even a celebratory ribbon cutting to celebrate the demise of the tragic death trap.

"It was declared the end of dead man's curve," noted the acclaimed Clermont County, Ohio author, historian, researcher, and writer Richard Crawford in the Dark Figure Productions video: *True Ghost Stories from Ohio with Richard Crawford.*

If only that proclamation had been accurate. Tragically, the month after its "safer" alternative had been completed, a 1968 Impala carrying five teenagers was pummeled by a '69 Roadrunner. It was said that the Roadrunner was pealing at them at speeds of over 100 mph.

The result was horrific and deadly; only one survivor (a male teen named Rick) lived to tell the tragic tale. It's been said that ever since that accident that crisp fall day, the four-lane intersection has been the site of a haunting by an otherworldly "faceless hitchhiker." This thumb-cocking fellow is witnessed as a dark black silhouette—like a three-dimensional shadow—of a man.

"This is regarded as the most haunted site in the state of Ohio by many people," shares Crawford on the video. "This place gives me creeps more than any other place I've ever visited in this county. I don't know how to describe it, but if you come here at night, this intersection is pitch black; it's like no intersection you'll run into."

There truly have been countless tragic, unexplainable events around Dead Man's Curve. Since its inception, the tally of victims at the site was off and running and has continued each year with over seventy people killed there and no signs that the end of the carnage is in sight.

"It's not just cars," says Shane Reinert, Dark Figure filmmaker. "Even when wagons were the main source of travel, there were numerous accidents and deaths." There is an extended history of tragic travel.

Crawford has witnessed something incredible on that stretch of road (more than once) as have others who have traversed it late at night. They see what looks to be a man, a three-dimensional shadow person with all of the appendages in tact, except for the fact that this being has no face. This creature is called the shadow man and, according to Crawford, he is always seen between 1:20 and 1:40 in the morning.

People who are driving that time of night around Dead Man's Curve might see this strange being walking along the side of the road; or their car might be pelted with rocks and/or the shadow man might literally jump out in front of an unsuspecting driver's vehicle only to be "hit" and then leap up and race after the car. At first glance, the man seems normal enough; it's only when folks get close enough to get a good look at him that they realize there are no eyes, lips, or nose to be found: no trace of a face. He also can seemingly disappear at will.

This deceivingly peaceful-looking road located at State Route 125 and 222 in Ohio is widely (and rightly) known as Dead Man's Curve.

On the video, Crawford recalls a time when his friend came running out of the woods after "doing his business," late one night. The friend was frantic, saying a bear was after him. "There's no bear in Clermont County," Crawford said they told him, but the friend was adamant, saying something on two feet was chasing after him. The group then saw something emerge out of the woods—and it was on two feet all right, but it wasn't a bear, and it had no face.

Crawford would give tours of that area and indicated they would often see ambulances around. There would also be random cars sitting there, and one time, the group saw a hearse, which followed them into a friend's driveway. It was 1:40; the car turned its lights on and ignition on and backed out, and the lights across the street showed that nobody was driving the hearse—at least nobody that they could see.

"The Shawnee say that the intersection was built over one of their cemeteries," Reinert added. "That could explain some of the problems. I've witnessed at least three accidents there, myself. It happens all the time and so many times they are fatal."

Both Reinert and fellow filmmaker Andy Crosier attest that many of the haunted sites they've filmed for their series have had some connection to Native Americans and a disruption of their burial grounds.

Several psychics have labeled the shadow man as being "very angry" said Reinert. Crosier and Reinert refused to visit Dead Man's Curve during 1:20 to 1:40 am because they are honestly afraid of what they might witness. Great documentary movie material to be sure, but they both agree that it just isn't worth the risk.

Reinert gives an example of said risk. "A woman who was working at Children's Hospital had to come back through Bethel to come home—she had worked a double shift," he notes. "She was driving in the station wagon she'd borrowed from her parents (she was going through a divorce or something) along 125 and she saw a guy on the road. The guy leapt out in front of her car and she ran over him."

"She got out of her car to check and sees the guy climbing on top of her car," says Reinert. "His hands were hanging onto her luggage rack." Obviously freaked out, the woman dove back behind the wheel and squealed off for home. Once there, she had her parents check the car. No sign of damage to the car, or of the shadow man was present.

In other accidents that happen there, said Crosier and Reinert, people swear up and down—even to the license plate number—that they can see that Green 69 Road Runner there, parked on the roadside. That exact vehicle has also been seen traversing the roadway; all the while with the driver's seat seemingly stark empty. Men and women have also claimed to see the car looking as immaculate and pristine as it did before the horrific accident occurred decade's prior. It seems that an Impala, too, has periodically been seen at the intersection—also without benefit of a driver behind the wheel.

Believe what you will, but with the numerous shadow man sightings, driverless cars and deaths at Dead Man's Curve, it would be wise to avoid that stretch of perilous road; especially between the hours of 1:20 and 1:40 in the morning. If you ignore the warning, you're doing so at your own (very real) risk.

Dead Man's Curve is located at 125 and 222 and Bantam Road in Clermont County, Ohio.

Habits Café in Oakley, Ohio.

Chapter 6

Habits Café In Oakley

Habits Café in Oakley, Ohio, is not your typical restaurant and bar. In addition to being a fine place to enjoy a wonderful meal of the freshest burgers around and a host of unique specialties, there is a lively (and deadly!) history connected to the site; a history that still seems to be hopping.

Step inside and you can't deny that Habits has an atmosphere of friendliness and a nice lack of pretension. You can play a game of pool or shoot some darts while enjoying a cold one and waiting for your dinner, or just stop in to kick back and relax. It's comfort food in comforting surroundings; perhaps that is one of the reasons they have a visitor or two from beyond that refuses to leave the premises.

Mark Rogers, who has owned Habits Café for years, said that in the 1940s the building was owned and operated by the Irish Mafia. Given that fact, it's not too surprising to hear that illegal gambling regularly took place in the basement. This morsel of information was confirmed to Rogers when the great grand nephew of the former bar owner strolled in and confirmed the specifics with him one night.

Legend also has it that a crooked police officer was gunned down in the basement and the former owner of the building was also shot and killed out in the back street of the pub several weeks later.

This building's flamboyant history, coupled with a menu of strange incidents, have all but convinced many of those who have worked there that there's something paranormal going on. Hearing the rumor about ghosts can be rather fun and exciting, but first hand experiences of the paranormal kind can be downright shocking.

Just ask Miss Joann Moore; the no-nonsense, ingratiating longtime cook at the café. About five or six years ago, Moore went to fetch some supplies from the cooler in the depths of the underground structure. She wasn't down there long, she recalls, when she saw a "real bright light in the other room." "I knew I was the only one down there," says Moore, "but still, I hollered out, 'Is anybody down here?'" No (verbal) answer ensued, but the bright light ("like a flashlight"), as if responding to her query, zoomed directly toward Moore's location. It was right about this time that Moore opted to bolt up the stairs.

"It was following me!" Moore says. She emerged from the basement confines shaken, but greatly relieved to be out of the dark belly of the restaurant.

Still flustered, Moore hurried into the café's kitchen, sailing right past the waffle iron, which had been plunked atop a top shelf a year prior. Suddenly the appliance flew off of the shelf, crashing to the floor behind her. Had this happened two seconds sooner, it would have landed right atop of her.

"It just missed me," she says. Obviously shaken even further, Moore hurried down the kitchen aisle only to then witness the clock, positioned high up on the wall, fling off and land right before her feet. The timepiece received blunt force injuries, but a determined Moore hung its battered face right back up (it didn't get the best of her!) and it is still hanging there today.

This is a fine example of Moore's spunk and vitality. She doesn't relish going back into the basement since that hair-raising light show and kitchen calamity occurred, but if she's alone and needs supplies, she will do so (albeit quickly). This is particularly amazing considering that after the aforementioned incident, Moore had somehow gotten locked down in the basement. Who or what did this to her is still unexplained, but it definitely took far too long for people to hear her cries and pounding to open the door. Were some paranormal entities playing a joke?

You would think these experiences might be enough to cause Miss Joann Moore to hightail it right on out of Habits, but you'd have to think again. She's staying put. Moore is not the type of woman to let someone or something scare her away. Nevertheless, she admits she does not underestimate what happened to her. It was truly frightening and it changed her outlook about the paranormal—and that dreaded tavern basement.

"Until you experience it yourself…you don't know how you'll feel," she says. When it comes to strange experiences at Habits, Moore is not alone. Rogers' son, Aaron, had his own haunting experience at the restaurant. "I am an atheist," Aaron says. "I don't believe in the supernatural." Yet Aaron vividly remembers what he saw, and reminiscing about it brings back how inexplicable and frightening it was.

The strange occurrence happened when Aaron was about seven years old. He and a buddy of his were playing downstairs at the restaurant basement. He explains that he would often run around the entire place, playing and exploring…typical kid stuff. Playtime turned into terror time for the young boy, however. "I turned the corner and looked across the length of the basement," says Aaron. "And there was this guy standing there—dressed all in white. Everything was white…his shoes," Aaron pauses. "Everything. Everything! Even his face."

Aaron thought for a second that he might be imagining it but realized he wasn't when he saw that same terror mirrored on his friend's face.

"It freaked us out totally," says Aaron. "The guy [apparition] saw us and he ran [up a second set of stairs], and we ran the other way!"

The two boys reached the top level in record time, out of breath and frantic. They told Mark Rogers, Aaron's father, about what they had seen, including the fact that this guy was floating several feet above the floor. Thinking there might be an intruder in the restaurant, Rogers immediately raced downstairs to investigate.

Despite searching every nook and cranny of that basement, he found nothing out of the ordinary. The doors were locked, so he knew nobody could have gotten in or out without him or his staff knowing it.

Rogers grins slyly when asked if he believed his son and his friend had truly seen a ghost. "There was no question that they saw something," he says.

Rick Barnes, a highly successful soundman that has worked on movies and television shows for many major networks is far more of a skeptic than a believer in ghosts. Yet Barnes will not deny that there was definitely something inexplicably strange going on in

2001, when he and a film crew were filming a scene for the independent movie *April's Fool* in the basement of Habits Café.

"I ran audio, and I ran it on batteries because there were not
a lot of electrical outlets in the basement," says Barnes. He went
on to say that the basement was "perfect for the shot" that they
needed in the film. The crew had just begun shooting a scene down
in the bowels of Habits when the cinematographer yelled, "Cut!"
The rest of the crew had no idea why.

**The basement hallway in Habits was where Aaron and his friend saw the hovering
man, clad in white from head to toe, with a blinding white complexion to match.**

"Didn't you see that?" the cinematographer asked. Nobody
had. They assumed it was something called a lens flare and began
anew. Soon the cinematographer again yelled, "Cut!" —this time,
because his batteries had died. He put in brand new batteries to
finish the shot, recalls Barnes, whose own set of batteries then
died. "You've got to understand; these batteries literally never
fail," says Barnes.

That might be generally true, but not so in the basement of
Habits. The filming began anew only to have the crew suddenly

witness "a flash of blue light," says Barnes. "It was almost like a spark and we all saw it this time." That meant it could not be a lens flare. A production assistant opted to head for the hills (aka, the stairs) quickly at this venture in the shoot, Barnes recalls with a chuckle.

The crew knew something out of the ordinary (and perhaps paranormally) was going on but they also knew they needed to get the shot so it would match up with the previous scene.

"So I ran AC from upstairs to finish the shot," says Barnes. The blue streak of light was not detected on the film—even though the entire cast and crew had witnessed it; this further attested that it was not a lens flare, Barnes says, because lens flares do appear on film.

"What just happened was impossible," Barnes adds. He has since been soundman for several national haunting-type shows, but says that the basement of Habits was one of the few places he was in that he believes has something unexplainable going on.

Habits Café has had other employees venture into the basement only to emerge shaken and with their own story to tell. Imagine a female employee's surprise, for example, at being vigorously pelted with rolls of toilet paper while trying to retrieve some supplies from the walk-in fridge. She saw nobody there, but the rolls kept flying her way. (Hopefully, the toilet paper was the extra soft variety.)

"It seems to show more to women than men," says Brian Robbins, General Manager of the restaurant. Yet Robbins admitted that he has, at times, seen a shadow or a glimpse of a fellow, who always seems to be wearing a baseball cap. Other employees have seen the same guy, too, he notes.

Who could the ghostly fellow in the baseball cap be? Who knows? Could it be the former bar owner perhaps?

Moreover, what about the dapper fellow in the blinding white zoot suit—with a powder-white complexion to match? Could it be one of the Mafia men that owned or frequented the joint when it was a gambling establishment?

Nobody knows who the entities are for certain. All they know for sure is that it's wise to request the made-to-order burger—and to expect the unexpected while visiting Habits.

Habits Café is located at 3036 Madison Road in Oakley, Ohio.

The Hammel House Inn, Waynesville, Ohio.

Chapter 7
Welcome to the Hammel House Inn

A sense of timeless history and warmth surround the Hammel House in Waynesville, Ohio. Visitors come from all around to stay at the charming inn; and it is often quickly apparent to some perceptive travelers that several ghostly visitors have never left. The innkeeper, Pam Bowman, shares the stories of her more "unusual" permanent residents with a wide smile and obvious respect. Whether it's the pitter-patter of tiny, ghostly paws, a young old-fashioned server girl in the kitchen, or the fluid movement of a shadow of a man, the Hammel Inn has their share of interesting otherworldly occupants.

The Hammel House Inn has had several incarnations. It is now a bed and breakfast, restaurant, and a gift and antique shop. The historic site, however, once housed the original cabin, a tavern, and bore the name, The Hotel Gustin. It also served as a boarding house and apartment building.

People have lived there, died there, and certainly had a rip-roaring good time there. The frame of the inn that stands today was erected in 1817, and the inn has seen several remodels. Enoch Hammel bought the building in 1844. He topped it off with a third floor ballroom, which was eventually taken down. Two families took it upon themselves to revitalize the building in 1987.

"The cabin on this site in 1787 was one of the first polling places in the county," says Bowman. "Actually," she adds, her voice lowering and smile growing, "Hammel House used to be a really bad place. A Quaker lady described it as 'bacchanalian revelry and ribald behavior.' She used to park her wagon in front of her cabin so her children couldn't witness it. It was a real rowdy place at that time."

Bowman felt a connection to the building long before she and her husband even purchased it. "It just emanates history and it's a great place to come everyday to work," says Bowman.

Bowman readily admits that adjusting to running a business in a building that is occupied by a couple of paranormal residents took some getting used to, at first. "In the beginning things would fly off the shelves and there would be breaking stuff," says Bowman. Despite this onslaught, the innkeeper stood strong and didn't retreat. That brave stance has paid off.

"We're taking very good care of their building. We love being here (and they know it)," says Bowman. "The building is full of a lot of happiness now. They picked on us a lot when we came here, they really did. It was like an initiation for us."

That isn't to say that the ghosts don't have fun with some of the crew. "There was a girl that was new here," says Bowman. "She was cleaning the building and she'd be up cleaning the fan, and then she'd come running down the steps—'he's up there again!'" Bowman laughs. "If you get a *scaredy cat* in here, they'll show up."

Bowman laughs because she knows the feeling well. "I was horrified to go into our basement when I first came here," she admits. "Lights would go off, [noises would be heard], but now we're fine. I'm not afraid to go down there."

Nevertheless, something/someone (?) is still hanging out down there, albeit nothing/nobody that's frightening. "When I first came here, we had a honeymoon couple that was traveling through the area visiting haunted houses. They asked permission to go down to the basement to take photos. [When they came back up] I asked them if they'd seen anything and the couple said, 'No, it's not haunted.'"

According to Bowman, the couple then retreated up to their room, but she was surprised to see the duo soon come flying down the stairs. They thought there had been an earthquake. Their whole room shook, but the rest of the building didn't. Perhaps this event changed the couple's mind about whether ghosts were at the inn or not. Bowman's not quite sure because they checked out immediately!

According to Bowman, one of their more popular ghosts is the shadow man. He might sound a bit frightening at first, but he's actually quite the opposite. Seems his greatest joy lies in making the employees of the Hammel Inn duck. It's as if something is coming at them from somewhere and the impulse to suddenly drop their heads follows. "Sometimes you'll duck. You don't think about it, you duck," Bowman shares. It often happens while the employees are in the basement; but not always.

Visitors witnessing the behavior in the upstairs hall might wonder if it is some sort of tic—or perhaps a new dance. If it were, it'd probably be called the Shadow Man Dance.

"It feels like something is going to fall right on my head," says an employee. It's obviously a strange sensation. "I wondered why I was ducking."

There are other signs that the Shadow Man is dancing around, as well. "We've heard furniture move up here," the employee adds, and she says that she and a coworker came up to check but nobody was there and no furniture was out of place. The shadow is in the shape of a man and he is dark all over. Those who do see him detect no clothing, said Bowman. They do not hear any sounds from the shadow. Instead, they'll see something out of the corner of their eye or walk into a cold spot.

"He's like a vapor," she says. "I've never seen the shadow face on." It seems that the Shadow Man particularly enjoys visiting rooms four and five at the Hammel Inn. "People actually request these two rooms for that reason," says Bowman. "He's not frightening. He kind of [sashays] between people. We've had ladies that have had slumber parties here that say he actually weaves his way in and out of the group. He's very comfortable here."

Bowman goes on to explain that the Shadow Man is attributed to the legend of the Hammel House. "He's been here a long time, and I think he just enjoys the guests at this point," Bowman shares. "There are two theories about who the shadow man is. The legend goes that there was a young gold merchant traveling through the area, and in those days he'd be equivalent to a jeweler in our time. He had lots of gold on him and he arrived with a beautiful team of horses and dressed very nicely," Bowman pauses and adds, "He was never seen after his arrival."

The legend goes that it was Enoch Hammel who was the innkeeper at the time, who did away with the young traveler. After all, it is documented that Hammel sold the travelers horse and carriage. The local museum has more research, however, says Bowman, and according to them, it was the innkeeper who owned the building before Enoch Hammel who actually murdered the traveler and put him in one of the wells behind the Hammel House. In fact, it was said that the innkeeper later made a confession on his deathbed that he did, indeed, murder the merchant. Even though the body was dumped into a well, Bowman assures the author with a grin that they use city water now.

"There are also two theories about our ghost," Bowman notes. "That it could possibly be the innkeeper because he's afraid to move on because of what he did; or it is the traveler because he doesn't really know what hit him." Regardless of how he came to be there, he doesn't seem to have any intention of leaving. "The shadow has made this his home," says Bowman. "He really has. We kind of share space here now."

The Shadow Man is not the only permanent resident of the house either. A particularly realistic-appearing paranormal member of the feline sector is also well represented at the inn.

"We do have a [ghost] cat," Bowman shares matter-of-factly, "which is probably our most active apparition. He looks so real, and a lot of times he sits right at the front door so when our bed and breakfast guests come in after dinner or something in the evening, he's sitting right there. I've had our guests ask me the next morning at breakfast where the cat sleeps."

People have watched the cat race up the stairs and have followed him up to the landing, but they are never able to catch him, nor able to see where he has disappeared to.

The surprised look on their faces must be priceless when Bowman tells the cat-sighting visitors the truth: "Well, we have no cat. We absolutely can't have a cat because of the restaurant and health codes."

The ghost feline not only looks real, but also seems to shed real, too—and quite abundantly. "We clean up small hairs every day off the carpet on our steps. Every day there are those tiny little hairs," Bowman says. "It's aggravating, but at this point, we're so used to him."

The kitty has another means of announcing his presence as well. "Sometimes you can smell him," says Bowman. "We've had guests come to us and say they wanted to change their room because their room smells like cat. They come back in later and the smell is totally gone."

"We've seen him in chairs and on the table. I've only seen him once, though, and it happens so quickly that you think, 'Did I see that?' I went to pull out a chair in the dining room and the chair was heavy." Bowman soon discovered why: the cat was "sleeping" there.

Although the guests and her employees say that the cat is black, Bowman says that the cat she saw was dark gray. Perhaps there's more than one feline at the Hammel Inn?

In addition to the Shadow Man and the kitty (or is it kitties?), there is one other paranormal visitor, that of a young girl. "She's only been seen twice in five years and she looks like a serving girl; we see her in the service area," says Bowman. "I saw her when I first came and it was so quick, but I remember her so vividly," she says, adding that she's not the only one who has seen her, either.

"We had this young man who was a temporary dishwasher for the day and he came back into the kitchen area and said, 'Ah, ah…there's girl in the serving area,' and I said, 'Okay, what does she look like, honey? Okay, you saw her, too?'" Pam's laughter fills the second floor hallway.

This vibrant innkeeper is sublimely comfortable in this historic building and it shows. "In the beginning, it was unsettling and I think they tried to unsettle us, I really do, but now they even have a sense of humor at this point," she says.

An example of their prankishness comes from Bowman. "Last year when I was getting the shop ready for Christmas, I was here very late and I had hung a wreath up on the soffit and walked away (probably twenty feet) and I had my back to the wreath. I was fixing stuff, rearranging something, and the wreath [flew off the wall and] hit me right in the hind end." Bowman laughs. "It was like they were saying: 'Lock the front door and go home. You have been here long enough!'" Bowman took their cue and took her leave.

**Paranormal visitors have been photographed on the inn's charming veranda…
and who can blame them for hanging around?**

"We have people that come back time and time again; they enjoy the experience," says Bowman. Guests have even snapped photos that contain faces of a man and a young girl on the outdoor veranda. "We've had several paranormal groups ask to investigate the place and we've refused. [They've even refused nationally televised groups.] We don't want to rile [the ghosts] up. They've been here a lot longer."

The inn does, however, offer Ghost and Goblet Dinners every weekend in October. Guests have dinner and then take a tour of Waynesville afterward.

Should you opt to spend a night at The Hammel House Inn, remember to bring your appetite, your camera and your ducking, er, dancing shoes. You never know who might come out to play.

The Hammel House Inn is located at 121 South Main Street. Web address is: www.hammelhouseinn.com.

Chapter 8
History & Hauntings = Home

Hauntings seem to follow Sarah*, a woman from Maysville, Kentucky and her adult daughter, Krissy*. Seems that wherever they each choose to put down roots, ghostly actions soon follow. The pair now resides in a Maysville home together that holds many rich secrets and, perhaps, souls from an incredible and historic past. The foundation of the house was built in 1794; it was the first courthouse built west of the Allegheny Mountains.

"There's a lot of history behind this place," says Sarah. "They used to sell slaves on the front yard. Harriet Beecher Stowe, whose museum is down the street, was visiting a doctor and watched the slaves being sold. Consequently, it was her inspiration to write the book, *Uncle Tom's Cabin*."

Sadly, the courthouse was struck by lightning and burned down in 1909, Sarah shares, and she hadn't yet uncovered when it was replaced, but figures it was probably around 1915 when it was rebuilt as a private girls' school.

"I am not afraid of ghosts because the last house I lived in was swarming with them," says Sarah. "I figured [the Maysville house] had to be haunted. All old houses are," she adds with a grin.

Her paranormal "welcome" arrived soon after she stepped across the threshold as the owner. "When I was first unpacking in the dining room, somebody came in and laid their hand on my back," says Sarah. "I knew." Sarah is a businesswoman who has run her own company for many years and she runs her household much the same way: Just as she sets ground rules on the job; she has ground rules for the ghosts.

"I always say, 'Look, you're welcome to stay in my house, just leave me alone, and do not ever, under any circumstances, appear to me in the middle of the night at the foot of my bed,'" she says.

"Right after I moved in there was a shadowy figure that stood at my bedroom door and that's the ghost that I know is there," says Sarah. "He's a very tall man, dressed in a heavy kind of huge coat with a hat. I couldn't see his face. The message I got from him was that he was hung from a tree in the front yard, or something happened at the courthouse, and he was not guilty, and he wanted me to clear his name." Sarah has not had the time to research the home, nor the events that occurred inside, while it was a courthouse, however.

Her daughter, Krissy, has experienced things within the house as well. She has heard doors open and close and found the metal cord from the ceiling fan wrapped tightly around one of the blades in one of the bedrooms. She asked her mom if she'd done it (she hadn't) and even tried to recreate it but couldn't get it to wrap around tightly no matter how hard she tried.

That's not all Krissy's witnessed. She has also seen a smoky fog in the hallway of the house and has noticed someone/something out of the corner of her eye. The "something" walked into the kitchen through the doorway.

"It really scared me," says Krissy. "It almost gave me a heart attack." She adds that there "have also been nights that I feel like somebody in the kitchen is watching me." Her mother concurs that she, too, has experienced the same reaction in the kitchen.

The Maysville ghosts enjoy messing with the plumbing, too; enough to cause damage. Sarah recalls coming home from a trip to Lexington only to find the hot water tap in the sink in the downstairs bathroom running full force. It had been running for four or five hours. In addition, the hot water tap was turned on for hours upstairs on full force.

"I talked to the plumber, because I'm a builder," say Sarah, "and he asked what type of faucets I had. He said with the type of faucets I had, that there is no way in the world that it could build up pressure, and that those faucets would turn on." Sarah found a leak later in the main drain pipe and she thinks that the hot water running for so long is what probably caused the leak in there.

The spirits seem to be curious creatures, as well. "This week I was really sick with a sinus infection," says Krissy. "I fell asleep on the sofa and something came and tapped me on the back—like three times. I turned around, and there was nobody there." Krissy shrugs. "That did not even scare me; I almost forgot about it," she says. "They just want to come and see what I'm doing and wake me up."

"I don't pay attention to most of it," says Sarah. "One of the things that is always missing, however, is the remote control."

Krissy, ever-the-daughter, quickly pipes in, 'No, I don't think they're stealing that; you're just losing it." The two women share a grin.

Despite the remote controversy, the pair agree that something/someone is hanging around that house. Sarah hears footsteps going up and down the stairs when she's the only one home, and a friend of hers, who stayed at her house for a time had his own experiences.

He was staying in one of the bedrooms upstairs, and he used to hear little girls playing, she says, adding that she figures that would likely be traced back to the time when it was a girls' school.

Sarah reiterates her familiarity with ghosts; the San Diego house that she occupied had seven of them; all so distinct that she named them.

The mother and daughter do seem to be more in tune with the spirits around them than most. Krissy lived in a northern Kentucky house that had its own share of paranormal residents, for example. The home was built in the 1800s and Krissy would sometimes hear a female voice whispering in her ear as she lay down to try and sleep. Her father, however, had the privilege of a full encounter with this lady of the night.

He had come to the area with Krissy's mom to help her look for a house. He was sleeping on the main floor, while the other two were sleeping upstairs. He was not one to live out of a suitcase—oh no! His clothes had to be meticulously hung up, says the pair, and so Krissy and Sarah provided him with a pole to hang his clothes on, which he took care of before he laid down for the night.

Sarah shares that the next morning when her ex-husband got up, he said, "My clothes fell down in the night. Who's that woman that helped me pick them up?"

"Nobody, there was nobody that helped you pick up your clothes," they told him.

"Oh, yes there was!" he insisted. "She had long dark hair and a white nightgown, and she looked really, really shocked that my clothes were on the floor; she even put her hand to her mouth. She was very nice and helped me pick them all back up and put them on their hangars," he insisted to his ex-wife and daughter.

"I told him, there's no woman here in my house," says Krissy, "but he would not stop talking about her the whole trip." Turns out that Krissy's house has already been sold several times since she sold it. "People don't stay in it longer than two years at a stretch," she says.

Sarah has her historic Maysville house up for sale now—not because of the ghosts, heavens no, but because she is downsizing her life. Neither Sarah nor Krissy would be surprised, however, if their next home comes complete with resident spirits. In fact, they'd be surprised if it didn't. They're both quite used to it, after all.

---

* Names changed for anonymity purposes.

Chapter 9
The Phantom of the Washington Opera

"**R**osemary Clooney may be the first lady of Maysville," notes Sean McHugh, "but Loretta Stambo's got to come in second!" McHugh, a writer and illustrator now living in Florida, is talking about the woman he and many others believe is haunting the Washington Opera House. McHugh was born and raised in Maysville, Kentucky, a plucky little historic town on the Ohio River, and he has a strong connection to this woman who long ago passed on but never seemed to depart. Loretta is so well known around town that she even had a play written about her (by Ann Parker) in the 1980s.

Maysville, located in northeastern Kentucky, has lots of little surprises to offer visitors, including the fact that they've had their own opera house for over 150 years. Located at 116 West 2nd Street, the Washington Opera House was initially erected in 1851, and now stands as the fifth oldest theater in America. Unfortunately, the structure perished in a January, 1898, fire. Its demise was short lived, however, because before the ashes barely had time to settle, The Washington Fire Company funded the $24,000 cost of rebuilding of the structure. The building was christened the Washington Opera House as a fitting result.

The beautiful layout has welcomed topnotch performers from around the U. S. including Marguerite Clark, Harry Garey, and John Phillips Sousa himself. The Maysville Players perform at the Washington Opera House periodically and special events are held there throughout the year, as well. Nobody's devotion can match that of the one, true, diehard performer, however. A dancer who loved the theater more than any other she'd pirouetted within:

and her name was Loretta Stambo. Loretta loved it so much that she's believed to have never left.

McHugh (creator of the *Broomsticks* young readers books) has had a lifelong passion for this woman of the theater in the town where he grew up. He has not forgotten his Maysville connections, and Loretta is a hands-down favorite of his. So much so, he sketched a headshot of the dancer for the author to showcase in this book.

Loretta still stays with McHugh, to this day. "I am a writer/illustrator of a children's book series," he notes. "Loretta actually makes an appearance in the Halloween story, "Broomsticks," *Book 2: The Halloween Spirit*, when my little witch and warlock meet Loretta. That's what kind of impact she had on me. It's no wonder I loved the whole mystery of investigating. Where I grew up, you could see the theatre, the graveyard behind the library, and Phillips' Folly.

How could I not be into this stuff? My friend, Kim Shannon, and I were obsessed and did so much research on the subjects that our librarian called us the Hardy boy and Nancy Drew."

"In the late 1800s, Loretta Stambo was a dancer (I always heard ballet was her thing)," says McHugh. "She wasn't from Maysville, but was with a traveling group and the Washington Opera House was her favorite place to perform." McHugh notes that Loretta was "very ill with pneumonia that fateful night, but always the trooper, went on with the show (regardless). She collapsed on stage but didn't die there, as some believe," he says. "They took her to her hotel on Market Street."

The Grave

"Loretta died at the hotel," says McHugh, "and her last request was to be buried in the theatre." A legend was born! Loretta was buried in the theatre in the dressing room under the stage. You can still see her grave today. They haven't touched it, not even during the restoration last year. No one walks on the brick grave out of respect. However, there is a story about an uninformed actor placing a Coke™ bottle on the grave, and when he did, it burst, spraying broken glass and coke everywhere. "I guess Loretta's a Pepsi™ drinker," quips McHugh.

McHugh had his own encounter with Loretta in 1979. "I was in the Maysville Players production of *Lil' Abner*," he says. "One afternoon, another cast member and I were working on the set. I don't recall the lady's name, but we were on the stage working when the lady said to me, 'Sean, could you bring me that piece of plywood?' Leaning against the wall was about an eight or nine foot piece of ply wood," shares McHugh, and "within seconds after the lady asked me for it—and before I could get to it—the plywood slowly fell over and landed beside the woman."

He goes on to explain that the wood "didn't come crashing down like you would expect something that size to do. [Instead] it glided down gently beside the woman. "The woman looked at me in shock," he recalls. "I looked back at her the same way. She [then] looked up toward the rafters and said with all seriousness, 'Thanks, Loretta!'"

Left:
**The Washington Opera House in Maysville, Kentucky,
is the fifth oldest opera house in the country.**

According to McHugh, "The one thing most of the Loretta stories have in common is this: She isn't an angry or scary ghost. She rarely does anything to spook anyone, but it seems she does expect respect."

McHugh does concede, however, that "most of the kind of scary stuff would happen after midnight if rehearsals ran late. Evidently, she wanted the place to herself after midnight. In fact, whenever I was in a play, I would have my mom call down to the theatre and tell them I had to be home by eleven-thirty. This was my idea, not Mom's," he recalls. "I wanted to make sure I wasn't there after midnight."

The Swinging Rope

McHugh says there are numerous stories about Loretta and one of the most told is that of the swinging rope. "It was one of those late nights," says McHugh. "All of the players had left but Shirley Toncray and Rose Leo (two ladies from the theater group). They were left to lock up. As they were about to turn off the lights, they noticed an extreme chill had come over the air. They also noticed a rope hanging from the rafters above the stage. It was slowly moving back and forth. Finding this odd, they walked up on stage and pulled on the rope. As they pulled it further down, they saw that it was hanging in midair. Frightened, they let go of the rope and it shot back up to the ceiling! Leo and Toncray have never been so terrified in their lives. "They left in a

Sean McHugh, a Florida artist who was born and raised in Maysville, sketched this rendition of the infamous, Loretta Stambo; Maysville's own, phantom of the opera.

hurry," says McHugh. "This account by them was recorded in a KET/PBS special that aired in the late seventies."

There are others in town that have their own strange accounts of a day or night at the opera house. Robert Roe is one of them. "In mid-May, 2007, the Washington Opera House was part of a city-wide youth festival which featured a morning talent revue and an evening concert," shares Maysville resident Roe. "Since I was running lights and sound for the performances, I stayed at the theater in between shows to get equipment set up. I was in the rear of the auditorium when I heard the sound of dress shoes walking across the stage from stage right. I assumed it was one of the Maysville Players board members coming in to check on the morning's performance. However, no one appeared on stage. I kept looking at the stage, waiting for someone to appear, then finally checked backstage. There was no one there. Actually, it made the Players' board of directors happy: Having just underwent a $3 million renovation of the Opera House, some people were afraid our resident ghosts might have moved out."

A Helping Hand

"A story I heard countless times, was when an actress was on stage rehearsing," says McHugh. "A heavy beam that was part of the set was hanging by a rope above her. The rope broke and the beam would have hit her—except witnesses say it moved out of her way as if by magic and then fell to the ground several feet away from the frightened actress." McHugh also relays that the theatre group commonly uses recordings for sound effects in plays, and on more than one occasion a passerby would spot the tape player running on its own "with strange noises coming from it."

An anonymous member of the Maysville Players recalls a specific incident in Halloween 2002. The Maysville Players were rehearsing in the opera house and without warning Rosemary Clooney's voice filled the theatre through the sound system. "It sounded like an old scratchy seventy-eight record. Other mikes were off and although all channels were tried, the music kept on playing. The radio station was called and they had not played any of Rosemary's songs that evening. People knowledgeable about the sound system were called and had no explanation for how this occurred. They had said it was impossible. Hey, nothing's impossible when the two "first ladies" of Maysville join forces.

The Portrait of Loretta

In the 1970s and 1980s, notes McHugh "there was a hand-drawn portrait of Loretta that graced a wall in the ballroom. It was just a headshot," he says. "She had dark hair pulled in a bun, 1800s style, and she had squinty, but powerful, eyes that seemed to follow you. I was always afraid to look at it, but once I did, I couldn't take my eyes off of it," he admits. "Very spooky; she sort of had a glamorous-looking Margaret Hamilton look to her. Underneath [the portrait]," adds Roe, "scrawled in black letters were the words, 'I Live.'"

"Legend has it that whenever they tried to paint over the portrait, [her portrait] reappeared." McHugh adds that "each time it came back, it had a meaner expression on its face. They must've found some powerful paint because eventually it was painted over for good in the late 80s or early 90s. I was appalled!" McHugh says, adding, "Who knows? Maybe it will reappear again someday."

Members of the theatre group, the Maysville Players, have heard and seen unexplained things in the opera house for decades. Many hear the telltale footsteps across the stage, like Roe did, others see a figure, dressed in black, while others have a sudden chill come over them, icier than the deepest January morn. Several have had the urge to exit the theatre immediately and have not known why.

Maysville takes their ghosts seriously, so much so that in 2004 they invited several clairvoyants into the opera house to see what spirits, if any, they would encounter. They encountered many; however, none of them were named Loretta. When asked if Loretta was there, one of the ghosts indicated, "A rose by any other name…" The clairvoyant believes that the woman people call Loretta is actually named Laura. After hours upon hours of research into the subject, however, McHugh would likely disagree.

"Just remember," stresses McHugh, "Loretta isn't an evil ghost. She just likes hanging around the theatre. Maybe her un-finished business was not being able to perform that night."

The Washington Opera House is located at 116 West 2nd Street in downtown Maysville, Kentucky.

Chapter Ten
The Creepy Coffee Table

Karen Barnett is a natural skeptic. "If there's a way to figure out why it cannot be paranormal than I will do my best to try and figure it out," the northern Kentucky resident says. In her quest to try and rationally explain the seemingly unexplainable, Barnett started a ghost hunting/aficionado group via an America Online forum a decade ago. In addition to hosting informative chats, they had a marvelous excursion to a haunted New Orleans B & B. Then marriage and foster kids took the front reign. When that portion of her life came to an end is when the paranormal events came to the forefront.

Family Reunion

One of Barnett's most incredible memories hails from 1996, when her grandfather paid her a visit. She was thrilled to see him of course, but quite surprised, as well, since her grandfather had passed away many years prior.

The time leading up to that sighting was a time of challenge and change. She had asked her husband for a divorce that year, but the couple agreed to wait to carry it out until their foster kids had left. It was probably seven or eight months after her divorce was final, Barnett recalls, when things started happening inside that house that she had lived in for years. Incredibly, all of the events that happened to Barnett occurred within the span of a single month.

"I was probably at the lowest part of my life when I saw my grandfather that night, and I really believe that that's why I saw him," says Barnett. "I was sitting in the living room and he was standing in front of me just as plain as day. He was just standing there, shaking his head." Barnett sighs. "And I just knew everything would be okay."

Blind Magic

It was a couple weeks later when Barnett experienced further paranormal phenomena in her previously quiet quad-level house. The structure was an open design with cathedral ceilings. The windows in the home were the slider type, which had no window-sills. One day she was on the lower level in her office working on the computer. The dog was in the room with her and she was busy typing away when they heard it. "It" was "the most awful commotion there was," says Barnett. She ran out into the hallway to see what had happened.

"My cat was standing on the first level, looking upstairs and his hair was standing up everywhere. He was like a big powder puff," she says with a laugh. Barnett quickly raced upstairs toward the noise and soon discovered what had caused all of the commotion: The mini blind that had been hanging in the bathroom was now lying all the way out in the hallway; a good twelve feet from that bathroom window.

"I put that blind up when we bought that house and it was snug," she says. "You know how when you put up the mini blind you have those two plastic pieces [in either corner] that slide in place over the blind?" she asks. "Well, those were still in place [even though the blind was down in the hall]."

Barnett went on to say that because there were no windowsills in the house, there was no way that the cat could be in the window—not to mention that her feline was downstairs with her and the dog the whole time, anyway. Plus it would be impossible for the cat to extricate the blinds and then slide those tabs back in place.

This anomaly really pestered Barnett. "I was trying to figure out for two days what happened in that bathroom," she says.

All Wet

Forty-eight hours later, while a storm brewed outside, Barnett says she was resting comfortably in her bedroom. She had her stereo system set up in her bedroom cabinet and it was connected to speakers throughout the entire house. Her stereo was an older model and the front button had to be pushed in to go *on* and pushed in again and out to go *off*.

About one-o-clock in the morning, Barnett received a rude awakening of the hard rock kind. The stereo suddenly blared on, full-blast. Not only that, it was tuned to a station she'd never heard of.

Shocked, she shot out of bed and turned it off (and yes, the button was in the *on* position). Unable to sleep, Barnett went downstairs and got something to drink. She brought her drink into the living room and slunk down on the couch with the lights off. Her nerves still raging, she lit a cigarette and tried to calm herself and somehow make some sense out of what had just happened to her.

"I'm looking at the coffee table which is about 2 foot by 3 ½ foot," says Barnett, "and I'm thinking, 'what in the world is wrong with that table?' and I reached over and turn the lights on, and the entire top of the coffee table is standing in water, like ¼ inch. There is no water dripping on the floor and there are no leaks in the ceiling," she says.

The most incredible aspect, according to Barnett is, "why wasn't it running over the sides of the coffee table? The magazines on the table were soaking wet. A quarter of an inch of water was raised up on that coffee table but not running over the edge of the coffee table." This is something that Barnett knows to be physically impossible.

"I didn't sleep at all that night. I cleaned it up and sat on the couch all night waiting, with the lights on, for something to drip on that table," she said. "Something to show me that I am not totally losing my mind!"

Dark Shadow

The very next night around midnight Barnett was working in her office. Finished, she started up the stairs, and as soon as she turned the corner, Barnett says, "I saw a solid black figure of a man running through the hallway."

As if that wasn't frightening enough, says Barnett, "Just then the phone rings, and I about jumped out of my skin." Who the heck would call at this time of night? she wondered. Turns out it was her very good friend Sandy calling.

Sandy is a Puerto Rican and Indian mix, says Barnett and, "she's very in-tune with a lot of things."

"What are you doing?" Sandy asked her friend.

"I said, 'I'm standing in the middle of my hallway freaked out.' Sandy asked me, 'What was that black shadow?" says Barnett, who stammered back, 'I have no idea.' Sandy said, 'I just want you to leave the house for tonight.'

"I don't have a problem with that," Barnett says she told her friend, and the northern Kentucky resident hopped into her car and hightailed it over to her parents' house. Barnett did return to her home, however, the next day. Moreover, she did so all by herself.

"I don't know how I was able to do that," admits Barnett. "I didn't talk to my mom and dad about it. I talked to Sandy about it and my sister, but I was fine because that next afternoon, I called Sandy and said, 'What do you suggest I do?' She told me some things I could do that involved sage and sea salt."

Barnett did as her friend suggested and never saw the shadowy man again. "What scared me was that Sandy later told me that whatever that was upstairs, she thought was more demonic than anything," says Barnett.

Barnett adds that she could tell by the figure that it wasn't her grandpa visiting her again. This figure was a different size and shape and very dark.

"The first few months back I didn't sleep very well," Barnett admits. When it was remarked that she was a strong and brave woman, Barnett replies, "Either that, or very stupid."

Looking back over the happenings of that month, Barnett is convinced something paranormal happened. "There was nothing I could do to explain it," says Barnett. "I try my best to figure out if there's anyway possible something non-paranormal caused it. I couldn't explain it. I couldn't explain it at all."

After those hair-raising weeks, nothing else happened in the house, which she continued to occupy alone for the next two years.

There have been a couple of things that have happened in the home where she now lives, as well, says Barnett, but nothing major. She doesn't remember any particular paranormal instances as a child, however, and her personality is such that she takes very much of it in stride.

Barnett understands that some of the strange, unexplainable occurrences (once they've been thoroughly checked out and labeled as such) are just a part of life. Instead of fearing that aspect, Barnett accepts it graciously, and is now a researcher and investigator with PINK (Paranormal Investigations of Northern Kentucky) where she helps others who are wondering if they might be experiencing paranormal signs, either by debunking them or confirming the presence of something from beyond. She's in her element, to be sure.

Chapter 11
Roller Coasters to Firing Rounds
The Town of Kings Mills, Ohio

The little town of Kings Mills, Ohio, is located about a mile up the road from the frenetic pace of Paramount Kings Island Theme Park. Two very different locations—one loud and raucous, the other quiet and sometimes downright creepy. Yet, if the stories are to be believed, both with their own other worldly visitors from the past: some of them so very young.

Amusement Comes in Many Forms

Paramount's King's Island Amusement Park is believed to have a ghost of a little girl that frolics around the tracks of the tram after night has fallen. "Sarah" has also been "seen" around the waterworks and skipping around the parking lot. They say this blonde, playful young female is clad in a bright blue dress and that she particularly enjoys appearing out of nowhere and causing people to slam on their brakes to avoid hitting her. It's rumored that she just might be buried in the small cemetery at the site.

It is also thought that a teenage boy ghost is hanging around the Eiffel Tower there. He is thought to be the spirit of a high school graduate who illegally climbed the tower and either fell to his death or was sheared in half by the rides cables. He is referred to around the park as "Tower Johnny." Johnny seems to get around, because some are quite convinced that the teen also haunts *The Beast* ride at the park as well.

According to the Forgotten Ohio Web site (www.forgottenoh.com), another paranormal park guest is Woody, recognized as a playful ghost who particularly enjoys frequenting *White Water Canyon*. Supposedly, his favorite pastime is to wreak havoc with the nerves of King's Island employees by tossing pebbles at the observation tower once night has fallen.

There have been deaths at the park over the years, including death by electrocution, and given the energy and the electric amplitude around the place it isn't a shocker that rumors about ghosts on site continue.

Paramount's Kings Island is located on Kings Island Drive off Interstate Highway 71.

Ghostly Ammunition

The Peters Cartridge Factory is a largely abandoned building nowadays, but back in its heyday, it was a bustling ammunition-making business filled with grateful town workers. The factory was erected around 1895 at 1415 Grandin Road, on a ten-acre site abutting the southern side of the Little Miami River. It was a darn impressive set-up back then and traces of its grandeur can still be seen. Well, sort of (if you look closely, or is it far away?) Many of the walls are bathed in graffiti and there are likely more broken windows than intact ones. There's just a general rundown ghost town feel to the place. Oh, and there are also ghosts.

The expansive site was where pistol and rifle cartridges, shotgun shells, and other smokeless cartridge ammunition were created. In 1934, Remington Arms bought the factory from Peters and continued cranking out ammunition until Remington consolidated and closed the Kings Mills location. Strangely enough, RCA's Columbia Records moved into a building on the grounds, and for four years, they concocted plastic materials and crafting records for phonographs. The building had other "lives" in the ensuing years, including being used as a warehouse for Seagram's Distillers and home to a cabinet company.

In the late 1970s, it was purchased by Landmark Renaissance Corporation, and the facilities were called the Kings Mills Technical Center. An eyeglass making company operated there and several other businesses as well. It's had a lot of lives working within its walls and, especially while it was a cartridge manufacturer, a whole lot of tragedies, too.

"A lot of people died here," affirms artist Greg Storer, who has kept his art and teaching studio in the smaller building in the back of the property for over thirteen years. "This is the primer facility," he says, "the most volatile place [in the entire plant]. They made primers here; there are still thousands of them between the floorboards."

Primers are the round-shaped balls placed within a gun cartridge that, when struck by a firing pin creates a spark that then instigates the powder charge. This is the action that propels the shot downrange. Lots of sparks, charges, and fires. No wonder employees were at risk.

Greg Storer is a painter whose studio is housed at the largely abandoned (and slightly haunted) Peter's Cartridge Plant in King's Mills.

Kings Mills was a "cool" town, notes Storer. "The company owned the church and built the town's houses (many of which look incredibly similar)."

Storer knew before he signed the lease that more than a few individuals had tragically lost their lives on the site that he was considering renting a space in, and he pondered how that might affect him and his artistic output.

"I had concerns about being here," admits Storer. He knew the reputation of the place, firsthand. "I would come out here in high school [to roam the building and grounds, even rumored then to be haunted]." The reasonable rent, coupled with the looming windows (in his studio they are in tact), however, convinced him that the space was too good to pass up. His art room soaks in the northern light, illuminating both the room and the colorful results of the painter's creativity.

"There's been rumors of cult and Manson family-type [activities here over the years]," says Storer, "but I don't feel any 'evil' energy. It doesn't frighten me to be here."

Storer has had a number of strange things occur at the site over the last thirteen years, but has no plans on leaving his beautifully-lit studio. It inspires him.

That's not to say that Storer doesn't think "some" type of vibration is hanging around. "There is definitely an energy here," says Storer. "I sense a heaviness, a beckoning energy; but I never get any weird energy." In addition to the "feel" of the place, Storer has had unexplained events occur, as well.

There have been multiple issues with the lights over the years. If he's sure he's turned them off before leaving, he will often come back and find them on. If he leaves them on while running a quick errand or stepping outside for a moment has he returned to find them off.

Storer compares the feel of the plant's environment to that which one might get when visiting a cemetery. "I get a graveyard kind of heaviness here," says Storer. Interestingly enough, the heavier aura of the atmosphere does not impede the prolific artist's output or focus. In fact, it's just the opposite.

"It helps me with confirmation that I'm doing what I need to be doing," Storer shares. He's not really quite sure how or why. The painter goes on to expound that being part of an artistic field can be very rewarding, but also incredibly challenging—especially in the monetary department.

For some reason the atmosphere at the former Peters Cartridge plant seems to encourage him to put paint brush to canvas and to not become too disillusioned.

Although he provides a detailed map and directions to his students before they set foot on the plant site, he's received his share of calls from first time students, often at the entrance to the overgrown, littered lot, asking him if they are really in the right place. He assures them that they are, and once they find their way back and enter the warm, enveloping studio, they quickly grasp the reasons why the sessions are held there.

Overall, it's turned out to be the perfect place for Storer to create. He definitely gets the feeling that he's not alone; even when he *is* alone. "Things move, doors creak," he admits, but he has never felt a "get out of here," vibe from the place. It's more like, "Thank God you're here," he says with a smile.

Update: Storer sent an email to the author in the wake of their meeting together. "After your visit, I started a painting about the spirits of Kings Mills," he wrote. "I guess talking with you stirred up some ideas. So this morning I am working on it, and I am thinking about how your visit, and the conversation about the presence I notice here has led me to this painting. At the moment that I completed that thought," continues Storer, "a large painting (on wood) that had been sitting on an easel behind me (about six feet away) for at least a week, crashed to the floor. There was no wind blowing, there was no one else here. This is the first time I have ever had anything move or fall," Storer wrote. "The painting was not damaged because it is on wood, but I will tell you, it gave me a bit of a chill."

The Peters Cartridge Plant is located at: 1415 Grandin Road, Kings Mills, Ohio. Greg Storer's Web site is: http://www.gregstorer.com/.

Now mostly a shell, the Peter's Cartridge Factory was once a bustling ammunition-making business in its heyday, largely employing much of the town of King's Mills.

Chapter 12
Lucy Runs...Forever

When driving in the town of Amelia in Clermont County, Ohio, it's a good idea to make sure you've got a watchful eye and an open mind—especially if you're meandering down the rural winding and narrow Lucy Run Road. Who knows? Wildlife might leap into your path. Then again, it might not be a deer, coon, or squirrel that you'll have to contend with. Instead, it might be a frantic bride, cloaked in a veil of white, rushing across the road to meet her lover. Romantic, huh? The only problem with this is the woman has been dead for well over two centuries and, more tragically, it was in the final minutes of her life that her lover left her for another.

Many people have claimed to see this young lady running across the road and disappearing into the grounds of Lucy Run Cemetery. The cemetery, and the road itself, now bear the name of this lovelorn spirit.

According to local legend, it is believed to be the ghost of Lucy Robinson, who drowned in the early 1800s while on a quest to reach her beloved; a man who left her for someone else.

It's been rumored that Lucy was the daughter of Charles Robinson, a fellow who had moved his family (which included several daughters), to the Batavia area from Maryland in 1797. Charles erected the family cabin on what is now the site of the Batavia Cemetery/Lucy Run Cemetery and positioned the family homestead beside a good-sized creek.

It should be noted that some believe that Lucy was actually a niece of Charles, not a daughter, but, regardless, it is the name of Lucy, which is connected with this legend. Whether she was Charles' daughter or niece, the girl was very beautiful and quite gifted. She seemingly had the world at her feet, and it wasn't long before a young man swept her off of them, and into his arms. The gorgeous young woman and her handsome suitor soon decided they were meant to be together forever and announced their engagement.

All seemed perfect for this radiant young fiancé until lightening struck—figuratively and literally. One evening, the man she'd pledged her heart and future to, bounded to the Robinson home atop his horse to speak with Lucy about a matter that could not wait. While he was talking to her, a raging thunderstorm barreled in. Hurriedly, he broke the news that broke Lucy's heart; telling her that he no longer wished to marry her because he had found true love with another. As the thunder rumbled and bolts of electricity hurled through the air, he abruptly turned and rode off, leaving a thoroughly dejected young woman in his wake.

She was likely brimming with disbelief and grief. How could this be? The proclamation from this man that she adored so very much came seemingly out of the blue. Desperately needing answers and, perhaps, to try and plead for him to rethink his decision, Lucy mounted her horse right in the midst of the maddening skies fury and dashed after the fellow into the dark and stormy night.

The rain pelted Lucy and her mount as mercilessly as the words from that young man whom she had so loved, her tears likely joining the liquid deluge from the sky. Mother Nature's fury was pouring forth in such a manner that maintaining her vision and composure was nigh on impossible. Tragedy was bound to occur and it soon did.

It was later deduced that Lucy was so disorientated by the force of the driving rain that she missed the bridge over the creek entirely, or that her horse lost its footing in the soaking wet muck and fell. Regardless of the precise cause, the outcome was the same. Lucy was tossed from her steed and landed in the thrashing waves of the roaring creek; its currents viciousness fueled by the incessant storm. She careened like a toy through the rushing waters and was swept away as the dark muddy water enveloped her and captured her last breath.

Shane Reinert, of Dark Figure Productions, was told that while noted author, historian and researcher Richard Crawford was filming a piece for a Dayton-area Television crew in Lucy Run Cemetery, a vision of Lucy herself sashayed right behind Crawford. "They didn't see it when filming," says Reinert, "but saw it later."

Since that tragedy occurred, the creek she drowned in has been known as Lucy's Run Creek and the land that trails beside it as Lucy Run Road. This young woman has been gone for over 200 years, but her white-clad form is still seen, draped in heavenly white garb, hurriedly crossing the road that now bears her name. Ironically, Lucy Robinson used to live in the cabin on what is now the Lucy Run Cemetery land, so in some ways, this poor, forlorn spirit has never really left home and never will.

Lucy Run Cemetery is located on Lucy Run Road in Amelia, Ohio.

Lucy has been seen in her white wedding dress on the road and inside this cemetery, both, which bear her name. (Note the white mist in the top, left-hand portion of the photograph.)

Chapter 13
Phillips' Folly

Mason County, Kentucky is a hotbed of history…and, if the stories are to be believed, hauntings. Innumerous African slaves fled a route through the rolling acreage to reach freedom, a route that was identified as the Underground Railroad. This trail included houses, churches, farms, false floors, tunnels, and secret, hidden rooms, such as exists in the Phillips' Folly home in Maysville—a large, stately structure believed by many in town to continue to harbor some of the spirits of those who once lived there.

African Americans often traveled during the blanket of night, tirelessly striving to reach what should have always been theirs in the first place: freedom. The Underground Railroad was successful because of those souls who worked together to help them cross the Ohio River to a new life. This network remained until Kentucky abolished slavery at the end of the Civil War.

Maysville, Kentucky, which is located about fifty miles southeast of Cincinnati, Ohio, is the county seat of Mason County. The pretty city rests on the southern banks of the Ohio River and, despite the inevitable aging and cracks in the facades of this small town, it has somehow kept its charm and sense of humor in tact. It has had brushes with fame: Rosemary Clooney was born there and is buried there. George Clooney is remembered as a teen that hung out on the corner.

Ferries port in town several times a week and cobblestone peeks out on some of the streets. Most everyone you pass offers a nod and a greeting. For a town its size, Maysville has a plethora of pertinent and incredible museums, some affording visitors the opportunity to step inside the shoes of a slave running for liberty—if only for the briefest of moments. It's an opportunity each of us should take. The National Underground Railroad Museum, led by Jerry Gore, is one of them. Freedom Time is the title of Gore's tour business and museum. Phillips' Folly is on his tour.

Imagine if a house were able to speak—cry, scream, and actually share its past with those who venture inside today. The sounds coming from Phillips' Folly would likely be sorrowful and heartbreaking. Maysville's second mayor, William Phillips, erected the twelve-room structure located on Third and Sutton Streets in the heart of Maysville in 1831. Along with six bathrooms and a butler's pantry, there was also a secret. A hidden room. Phillips was a slave owner, and the basement of his home held a cell where his slaves were kept.

There have been paranormal sightings throughout the massive house, but some people, such as Shelby Hanson believe it is that cellar that houses the majority of the hauntings. Hanson is a refreshingly candid and ingratiating resident of Dover, Kentucky (town next to Maysville) who had her own experiences in Phillips' Folly several years back when she ran her candle business there. She had been making candles for years and the thought of opening her own candle shop had been in the back of her mind for a while, but little did Hanson know that fate would end up leading her to do so in the historic cellar of Phillips' Folly building. The year was 2002 when the opportunity presented itself. Hanson knew from the get-go that it was something she had to do. "I have always been drawn to that place," she says.

"Shelby, you know that place is haunted," a friend warned her after learning of her plans. "Yeah, I know, but the dead don't really bother me; it's the living that do," she told her. This friend's brother had lived in Phillips' Folly and had moved out after only two weeks. Strange sounds, footsteps, and a *TV* with seemingly a mind of its own contributed to his quick departure.

This didn't bother Hanson. After all she was "drawn" to Phillips' Folly for years before she'd ever stepped inside. "I'm a history fanatic," she says. While she was deep in the midst of refurbishing her spot in the historic building, she came upon Jerry Gore at a local restaurant and asked him if he'd like to go see the cellar and the hidden room. "I knew the cellar was a place of interest for him," she says, and she felt compelled to contact him.

Phillips' Folly in Maysville, Kentucky, was a stop on the Underground Railroad.

According to Hanson, Gore was thrilled about the chance to finally get into that hidden room (someone had been living there before, so he had been unable to visit up until then). She said Gore told her: "The spirits have sent you to me." Gore met with her soon after, along with a group of his colleagues. He walked in alone at first, says Hanson. "It was very respectful. It gives me cold chills to think about it now," says Hanson. "It was a great thing."

"There's a lot of things that happened to me [in the cellar]," says Hanson. "We ripped up carpets, and I was on the floor, and I said 'David, look at me!'" He could see her breath. "'It's so cold over here!'" The chill came over her suddenly and left soon after.

"I wasn't afraid to be in there," she says, adding "that there were people who wouldn't go in the back room." Her daughter, who worked for her at the shop, had one hard and fast rule: "When it gets dark, I'm outta here!" Kids, especially, seemed to be particularly sensitive to the vibes in that area, and some completely refused to venture inside. "There's nothing back there to hurt you," she would tell the children.

"Many a time I felt something stroking my hair, or had a hand on my shoulder, like a handprint on my back, says Hanson. "I was like, 'okay, I know you're here,'" she says. Other people told Hanson that they would get taps on their backs and shoulders, too.

There was a potter who had some items at her store. One day, when she opened the shop, several pieces of pottery looked like they had a film over them. Thinking that was odd, she went over and looked; the pottery was ice cold and the paint was peeled off of it. Moisture? Maybe. Maybe not.

Another day when she was at the shop, she was stocking her wares as usual until something highly unusual happened. A sudden, intense emotion enveloped her.

"It was like when I went in there, I was going back in time. It was like a peaceful feeling," she says. "I can't explain it, but I got a whiff of joy over me and I mean I could envision this little short black lady, and I couldn't get her off of my mind."

"This is crazy," she says she thought. "I could envision her and she was just this jolly little soul. Right now I've got cold chills, just telling you this."

"Two or three times a week something odd would happen," says Hanson. "All the time, when I went in, there'd be a thing on my answering machine and when I would go to check the messages, it would be like someone was in the shop trying to make a call out."

Hanson says that she would "get the feeling" to play certain types of music that she'd never really listened to before. "It was like it put me more in touch with what I was dealing with down there, you know?"

Jerry Gore brought in a tape that was music back from slavery time and she enjoyed playing that often, as well. One time she heard a buzzing in her ear, like somebody "was whispering in my ear."

Once an employee of her friend who worked at the café came running up to Hanson and said, "I've just seen a dog!" The dog ran into the back. "I know she was scared," she says. The woman took off and didn't come back. Hanson went to try and find the dog, but she didn't see it. Turns out, there is a ghost dog seen periodically at Phillips' Folly. Unable to afford to keep her shop inside the place, Hanson had to leave the site. It breaks her heart to this day.

"Everything is not coincidence. I know something's there. I felt like that's where I was supposed to be. I wanted to be there all the time, but reality overrides…"

Ronna Kay Roe-Howard is an investigator with East Side Paranormal Society and they were in the Phillips' Folly house in April of 2007. "When you enter the basement from the side street, there is the first slave cell on the right," shares Roe-Howard. "When one of our women went into this room, she immediately had grief come over her. She cried and said that she felt totally helpless and sad in this room. As soon as she walked out of the room she was fine. She returned to the room later," Roe-Howard shares, and was fine.

The group used video equipment during the investigation and had some interesting footage emerge. "My son was viewing a copy of the video and he keeps hearing knocks, then a flash goes across the screen," says Roe-Howard. "He said that this occurred several times." Roe-Howard goes on to share that "just before we had done the investigation there, one of the attorneys on the first floor told me that there was a purple haze that was just above her head, and all of a sudden it went straight through the wall. Her secretary also gave us this account."

"Another story is of a man and his dog," Roe-Howard shares. "On a night of a full moon, at midnight, you can see him playing with the dog on the second- floor balcony." Roe-Howard has been on multiple investigations with the ghost-hunting group, and when asked which site she felt was most likely haunted, her answer was clear.

"Phillips' Folly was an awesome site, rich with history from the Underground Railroad," shares Roe-Howard. "I felt there were many residual spirits there." Many others seem to agree.

Visit masoncountymusem.org for further information on local tours and history.

This photo was snapped in the basement of Phillips' Folly. There is a feature of a woman with a white kerchief on her head, standing to the left of the photo, with her head turned away. There are also several white faces in the photo. *Photo courtesy of Ronna Kaye Howard.*

Chapter 14
Knock-Knock...Who's There?

"I'm unsure what is haunting my parents house," says Megan Simms. All Simms knows for sure is that *something* is hanging around that place and it is not of this earthly plain. Although she has heard plenty of strange things in the Burlington, Kentucky, residence, actually seeing an entity was a rare occurrence, but it did happen. It all began when Simms was a child.

Voices from out of nowhere

"When I was around six years old, I had answered the telephone and my uncle was on the other end, and he asked to talk to my Dad," Simms says. "I got my Dad and then went into the other room to play or watch *TV*. A little while later, I was looking for my parents and couldn't find them inside the house. So me and my older brother were looking outside for them. We saw them at the fence at the end of the yard. We both started running toward them. My older brother asked me why our mom and dad were walking together. Then I heard this loud man's voice say, 'Megan your grandpa's dead.'"

"I remember I stopped dead in my tracks and said to my older brother, 'Grandpa's dead,'" Simms notes. "We started running again and when we got to our parents, I said, 'Grandpa's dead isn't he?' My Dad said 'How did you know?'"

Simms then told her parents how she had heard that loud voice talking to her, "and of course, no one believed me," she says, adding, "That is the very first thing I remember that I couldn't explain."

Who are you?
"I have only seen one thing in the seventeen years I lived there," says the northern Kentucky lady. At that time I was about ten years old." Simms recalls that this happened when she was standing in the hallway, watching who she *thought* was her younger brother walking into his bedroom down the hall.

"It was evening when this occurred and the hallway was getting dark," says Simms. "My brother's bedroom is located directly at the end of the hallway, and when the door is opened, you can look directly into his room. This evening the bedroom light was off and his room was dark. I saw the back of my brother walk into his bedroom, so I yelled out his name and I got no response from him."

"I ran down to the end of the hallway and opened the door all the way so I could see in it," Simms shares. "He was nowhere in the room. I was standing in there all alone."

This defied what Simms had just witnessed. "I called out his name and got no answer," she says. "The hair on the back of my neck was standing up and I got goose bumps all over. I was freaked out, so I turned and ran out of the bedroom and all the way down the hallway. I ran into the family room and saw my brother sitting there on the couch. I asked him if he was just in his bedroom."

Her brother replied, "'No, why?' So, I told him what I saw and he didn't believe me," Simms says.

"I have always heard things in my parents' house," says Simms. "The first experience I had was when I was about six or seven years old. I was asleep in bed with my younger brother and our Mom. It was early morning—maybe six or seven am. I heard a loud banging noise that was coming from under the bed. It was the only noise that I could hear. The rest of the house was quiet and everyone else was asleep. I got scared because I didn't know what was making the banging sound. I was afraid to get out of bed so I stayed there very still and the banging stopped after thirty seconds or a minute; the banging didn't last very long. When everyone woke up later that morning, no one believed me."

Oh, Baby...

There have been other strange instances in that home. One morning when Simms was about twenty-three years old, she was in the bathroom, getting ready for work, and she heard something out of the ordinary for their household—the sound of a newborn baby crying.

"I was in the bathroom brushing my teeth when I heard [it]," says Simms. "I leaned down toward the vent in the floor and heard the crying get louder. My parents don't have a basement under that part of the house, but there is a small crawl space with a dirt floor. I got goose bumps all over my body and hurried up and left the bathroom. I went right next door to my bedroom and couldn't hear a thing. I had to leave for work, but later that afternoon, I asked my mom and dad if they heard anything, and my dad said that he had heard it before, the same noise I heard. No one else heard it that day, but my dad even went down to the crawl space to look under the house to see if an animal had babies under the house. When he went to look, he found nothing [there]. I got goose bumps all over again when my dad told me this," Simms notes. "I know very little about my parents house, but I do know at one time it use to be a big farm."

Years ago, it wasn't uncommon for people who passed on to be buried on their own land in a family cemetery. Such seems to be the case for this Burlington home. There are maybe six headstones along the fence line; somewhere possibly on their property used to be a cemetery," notes Simms. "The earliest headstone that can be read is from the 1700s and the newest is from 1800 and something. There are only maybe three headstones that can be read."

Over the years, Simms has shared these experiences with her family and some of her friends, but she says that she doesn't tell everyone she knows simply because some people are skeptics and "want me to change my story," she says. "They say, 'Well, it could have been this, or it could have been that.'"

Simms is a level-headed young woman who knows what she heard and what she witnessed, and she doesn't feel the need to defend her experiences with skeptics. It *was* what it *was*, as far as she's concerned.

Although Simms is the only family member to have actually seen a ghost, other family members have definitely noticed some out of the ordinary things in that Burlington, Kentucky, house. They've heard footsteps, a baby's cries, and there has been knocking on her brother's bedroom door (not done by a human hand).

"The footsteps are heard only at nighttime," she says, adding that she no longer lives in the house, but her parents still do. It appears that the paranormal sounds have not ceased with Simms departure.

"My mom heard footsteps one night two weeks ago," says Simms. On it goes…

Chapter 15
What are These? EVPs?

Ghost Hunting for the First Time

For many it sounds darn fun to go ghost hunting for a night, especially since you figure you can leave the ghosts where you found them (if you are lucky enough to discover them, that is) and return home to your quiet, ghost-free, respite. Imagine, however, moving into a Middletown, Ohio, house with your fiancé only to find that you can distinctly see, hear, and smell that "others" already live there, and seem to have no plans of taking a hike. (Hmmm, "several unidentified spirits living on site" wasn't listed on the purchase agreement, was it?)

Compounding this fact is that you husband works elsewhere and commutes home on weekends, so you are alone much of the time (sans *human* counterparts, that is). Unnerving? Could be. Your original plans are to remodel the 1859 home and update it to suit your lifestyle, but from the moment you first pick up a hammer, strange things start happening. Are you imaging that you heard those footsteps tromp up the stairs? Is this really the third day in a row that you've locked the back door only to come home and find it open? Did you honestly hear someone/something move heavy furniture across the upstairs bedroom floors when you're the only one home and, besides, there's no furniture up there to move?

PINK to the Rescue

It could be enough to make you question your sanity—at least a little bit. A friendly, concerned couple in their midyears of life, Jerry and Colleen, found themselves doing just that, wondering what had already moved into their century-plus older home before they did in January of 2007. To see if they were "hearing things" or actually hearing (paranormal) things, they contacted Mike Palmer of PINK (Paranormal Investigations of Northern Kentucky http://www.paranormalinvestigatorsofnky.com/) to find out.

"Nothing really bothered or scared me," says Colleen. "It just made me think for a minute I might be going a little crazy!" She laughs. "I must admit that while I am not really scared to be here, and I do not feel that the [ghosts] here are bad, I did get an eerie feeling."

No wonder: It would be eerie to smell something frying on the stove for dinner, even though you could see nobody in the kitchen cooking anything. And it would seem rather bizarre to find that the pantry door in the kitchen swings wide open on its own after it's been securely latched, and that the towels you set down in one place keep ending up in a completely different place. Toss in the fact that both you and your husband have seen a dark shadow flitting about out of the corner of your eye; on numerous occasions. Strangely enough you're on your third cable box in three months. Say what? The cable company doesn't understand what keeps making them go haywire but you have a vague idea. Problem is, you are afraid to tell them what your vague idea is. What would they think? Are they trained how to tackle paranormal cable interference?

"The more we remodel things, the more it happens," says Jerry, who was especially adamant that they figure out what was going on since his wife was home alone for so much of the week. Was it safe for Colleen to be there? He had to be sure of the answer.

Attempting to understand what makes the paranormal world tick is a difficult and elusive task. Seems that most everyone has his or her own opinion on what constitutes proof of activity and truly indicates an active haunting. In addition, people's unique perceptions and past experiences also directly affect their take on the topic.

Considering that this book is about Cincinnati and tri-state area haunted sites, it seemed only natural for the author to feel compelled to investigate, firsthand, how an authentic ghost hunting investigation is carried out.

Palmer has been at it for several years and was gracious enough to ask this author to chronicle an investigation at the aforementioned Middletown, Ohio, home. Brad Rubin of Paranormal Worlds was also invited to come partake in the investigation that summery Saturday afternoon, as did Karen Barnett, a researcher and investigator with PINK. Little did the hunters, or the author, know how incredibly active and intriguing this nondescript home would turn out to be.

It should be noted that the Middletown house was an anomaly in more than one sense of the word. The investigation was held during the day, for example. The reason was that the couple claimed that they noticed the majority of paranormal activity during daylight hours.

"That is really rare," says Palmer. Rubin agrees. The vast majority of their investigations are staged throughout the wee hours of the night when most activity is traditionally received by the residents and is more easily recorded with their special equipment.

The group descended upon the home and quickly got down to business. After a thorough interview and house tour with the couple beforehand, the crew set up loads of equipment including cameras, digital recorders, video recorders, and more. EMF (electromagnetic field) meters were utilized to try and locate a fluctuation in energy. The group also put dowsing rods to use and set up several recorders to try and collect any EVPs (electronic voice phenomena) around the house.

Colleen, Jerry, and some relatives and friends remained at the address while the investigation took place, but stayed outside in the large back yard so the crew could work to obtain accurate readings. The couple also covered the upstairs windows with blankets so Rubin's night vision equipment could be better utilized. Soon everything was set and in place. Despite some variant movements of the dowsing rods and a slight blurp on Rubin's EVP machine, the first portion of the investigation seemed quiet and uneventful. As the day wore on, however, the action began to pick up.

Palmer had heard that the homeowner had previously discovered a jar of some sort and a Bible in the attic, and he went to retrieve them. After perusing the pages of the holy book and the names and comments inside it, he returned up the ladder and pulled himself completely into the confines of the rafted, top portion of the house. Once he was up in the attic, bizarre things began occurring within the home. The second floor became a hotbed for orb activity, some of them on video seeming to play "games" with the investigators. In addition, while on the ladder, Palmer felt "something or someone" touch the nape of his neck four times.

(He was not present several hours earlier when the homeowner had told the author that when he had been on the ladder in the attic something had touched the back of his neck four times.)

Who says ghost hunting is glamorous? Mike Palmer, founder of PINK, crawled up into the attic of the Middletown, Ohio home several times during his investigation.

Can't Find Bugs? Let's Catch Some Rats!

The author brought along her digital camera and mini cassette tape recorder and was astounded when she replayed it later and heard several EVPs— One of which was also captured on Palmer's expensive video and digital EVP recorder. While Rubin was discussing having thought he heard "something" EVP-wise in the living room, but couldn't make out what it said, a voice came out of nowhere and said, "Schiller* (*name changed for privacy purposes)."

The other EVP the author came away with was a disembodied sounding male voice saying, "Can't find bugs?" This was overheard while Palmer and Rubin were discussing the lack of bugs in the attic (with respect to orb sightings).

"This is an example of a rare and solid EVP," Rubin notes. He also caught several other amazing EVPs. "In the upstairs bedroom near the camera, there was apparently an old pot belly stove; you can still see the pipe cutouts where it resided next to the doorway. In this (EVP) you hear what sounds like a match striking a few times until it catches, then a "sizzling" sound, which could be gas or grease cooking or even water. There's no plumbing upstairs and never has been though."

Is this the sound of someone lighting up the stove from long ago? Rubin heard the same sizzling sound again later while walking alone upstairs with his camcorder. He also caught a very strange (even from paranormal standards!) EVP: "Let's catch some rats!" Say, what? Not a typical EVP, that's for sure. What's interesting is that Palmer later in the attic discovered a dead rat skeleton. Rubin also recorded an EVP of a male voice saying, "Hi." This was especially pertinent to the investigator because he had just finished saying out loud, "Hi, is anybody here?" And Rubin also caught the inaudible (at first) conversation ending with a male saying, "Who's come up here?" Truly incredible stuff.

Palmer has video of an orb in the upstairs back bedroom that seems to be playing a game with him; moving around and waiting for his camera to catch up to it. Both Palmer and Rubin were in the attic at separate times and both came away with interesting evidence.

Rubin shares: "Mike and I both got somewhat similar ectoplasmic-like shapes flying around in front of us. I was in the attic and a long, ectoplasmic-like shape drifted up through the ceiling in front of me and disappeared out of the IR [infrared] range going straight up. I have no explanation at all for this, it's not a piece of lint or thread or insulation; if you pause it, you can see it broken up into three different shapes at one point, then it fades away and keeps going straight up."

The Shadow

Using his camera set to IR mode, Rubin caught what appears to be a massive shadow figure in the back upstairs bedroom. He's never seen anything quite like it and neither has Palmer. That bedroom, when we visited the site, had no door, yet still had the remnants of a lock that was once positioned on the outside of the door with the obvious intent to keep someone locked within. Frightening.

On his Web site, Paranormalworlds.com (where you the reader can go for future updates about this wonderfully haunted house), Rubin shares: "The 'Shadow Figure' video below, may never be 100% conclusive, but we felt good enough about it, that it would be worth putting up for people to look at. There are a couple of things to consider regarding it: the shadow 'materializes' suddenly, remains still for a second or two, then grows to a very large size and moves out of the camera. It has an ethereal quality with hard/sharp lines and a very solid black color. May resemble a curtain or Victorian era dress, hard to tell what it is. The clients had reported stories of black shadow figures in the home, or shadows." Rubin adds, "A bright orb accompanies the shadow. The only way a shadow would show up on that wall in IR mode, in that setting, would be if someone stepped in front of the camera (Rubin experimented with this to be sure). You'll hear no footsteps, either (you would if anyone even took a step up there)."

Given the plentiful and interactive EVPS, coupled with the rather convincing video evidence, Rubin credits the Middletown investigation as one of the most active he's ever been on, and Palmer agrees that the evidence they came away with was nothing short of fantastic. They are definitely returning for another investigation.

Rubin's results are documented as follows: "Active and most likely haunted with one or more local spirits. [There is a] very strong mobile energy present on upper floor. The nature of the activity does not seem to be hostile or frightening. Only male voices are heard on recorded audio. Some are residual, others are inquisitive or greeting or suggestive. They never appeared to be upset or agitated."

Palmer met with the couple several weeks after the investigation for the reveal and laid out the evidence the group had amassed.

Brad Rubin listens for EVPs and Karen Barnett puts the dowsing rods to use at the recent Middletown home investigation.

The Reveal

"I found it all very interesting. I knew that there was something going on here and that it was not all in my head!" Colleen shared with the author afterwards. "I was really hoping to hear a female voice, but just to hear something and know that I was not imagining things was a relief. Thank you all so much for proving it! It is so amazing—what you can do with all your equipment. Some of the things Mike showed us made me want to find out the history of this house even more."

Following the reveal, Colleen said she does believe she's heard even more sounds coming from upstairs, "but I honestly do not know if I am just wanting to hear it or if it's there, because, again, I experience these occurrences more when I am home alone. I have noticed that the plastic we have hanging at the bottom of the steps (to save heating and cooling costs, since nobody lives upstairs) seems to push out and stay like someone is just standing there, and I see my dogs just sit and look at that spot."

The pair are still going ahead with their plans to refurbish the house, especially the kitchen, bathroom, and updating the electric, says Colleen. "Mike did say that as we get further along in the remodeling, it may stir them [ghosts] up more."

The couple had initially told Palmer that they were going to renovate the house and then sell it, but they are already rethinking their decision to leave. "I love this house, what with the nice yard and the front porch and all; and I feel comfortable here." She adds, "When Mike left after the reveal, Jerry made the comment that he might be changing his mind about selling. So everyone keep your fingers cross that I get to stay here for a while…"

The most shocking moment of the reveal, says Colleen, is when Palmer played them the EVP that whispered Jerry's last name "Schiller*."

"It was a little upsetting to Jerry because that is his last name and we have no idea where that came from," she wrote. "I was already a believer in the paranormal and ghosts. This experience has made me want to dig deeper into the history of this house and find out all I can about it," Colleen adds. "I find that everyday I have more questions."

When it comes to her fiancé, the process has been an eye-opener to be sure. "As far as Jerry goes," Colleen says, he was not so much a believer (at first). He was more of the mindset that all things can be explained scientifically. However, he now sees things differently. He has come over to our side, so to speak."

Colleen is also fine with letting everybody in the house (human and otherwise) have his or her space. "I know that this was their house first, so in essence, I guess they are letting us live here. I probably shouldn't say this, but I think it bothers me that I have not (been able) to actually hear or see them yet. I talk to them everyday—call me crazy—and Lord knows that if they did answer me or if I did see them, I would most likely freak out, but I would like to see them. Being alone now in the house brings no worry or stress at all. "I am totally fine with it," she says. "I carry on conversations with them. I haven't got any answers yet…but I am waiting."

Colleen encourages those who are living in a similar situation, wondering if something paranormal is going on around them to have it checked out.

"If you think there is something there," says Colleen, "there probably is. Yes, have someone come and do an [investigation]. It is truly a great experience."

This author would most definitely agree!

* *Names changed for anonymity purposes.*

Chapter Sixteen
The Hook Man
of Pond's Run Road

There are a multitude of versions of the dreaded hook man across the wide divide that is America. In fact, it seems like most Lovers Lanes around the country have their own resident hook-wielding monster, poised to pummel unsuspecting amorous teens to death by swinging his piercing appendage viciously into their young, nubile flesh.

The Cincinnati tri-state area is no different. Legend has it that our area's hook man lives around Pond's Run Road in New Richmond, Ohio, and considering how far back the stories go, he's been doing so for many decades.

A Child Left Behind

The Pond's Run hook man tale begins with a very odd child who was the product of a doctor and his wife. The family lived on a hill overlooking Pond's Run Road in Clermont County. From the get-go this boy seemed to come from a "different" mold—one that was not only strange, but also impulsive and violent. This scenario was likely made all the more tragic for the father, whose career depended upon people trusting him for his medical prowess. Having a son that exhibited bizarre behavior just couldn't have been good for a medial professional's business.

Not surprisingly, it's been said that the doctor and his wife kept the boy as close to the house as possible; even sometimes tying him up in the basement so he couldn't get away and make trouble around the neighborhood… or worse. If you look at it from the kid's point of view, that would not be a very nice way to grow up. Toss in some added psychiatric issues because of the constant isolation and you've got the makings for real trouble, And if the legend is true, real trouble is exactly what occurred. All hell broke loose when a violent thunderstorm roared through New Richmond and lightening struck the family house and sparked a fire.

As their furnishings went up in flames around them, it was smoke that took the lives of the sleeping doctor and his wife, while their son was left chained and alone in the basement. The panic that engulfed him must have been unbearably frightening as his own death flickered closer by the minute. He was trapped.

Any screams that came forth would likely have fallen upon his parent's dead ears. It is rumored that their troubled son, now a young man, armed with a fit of sheer adrenaline fueled by terror, was somehow able to extricate himself from the metal tie binding his wrist, but only at the gruesome expense of leaving his bloody hand behind. In the wake of this rumored event, Pond's Run became synonymous with strange occurrences.

Howling and Growling

Following the storm, neighborhood canines suddenly became overtly loud and boisterous at nighttime in the Pond's Run area, and have yet to settle down. They howl at the woods and growl at nothing at all…or is it nothing? Items that residents left in their backyards would simply vanish; including food. There was repeated evidence that someone was living in the woods—empty food containers strewn about, signs that a fire had been lit, etc.—but no human being was ever glimpsed at these sites.

Even more shocking was the murder of a young couple that was said to have occurred at or near what once was the wooden bridge on Pond's Run Road. The report indicated that the lovers were stabbed to death with a pointy object, such as a metal puncher or ice pick or…a hook, perhaps?

This stirred the simmering pot of fear around New Richmond to boiling. Homeowners that lived right along the road up and left the area, no reason given, never to return even to this day. Entire rows of homes were torn down and were never replaced. Nobody that lived there will attest that they left out of fear or that they ever believed the hook man existed, but a feasible reason for such a large exodus from the area has not been forthcoming and is puzzling to many. All of this terror and unknown danger only heightened the fun/fear factor for the Lover's Lane devotees. It made it that more thrilling to go park out there. Crazy, huh?

These woods are the stomping grounds for the Hook Man of Pond's Run Road. Notice the dense blob of mist (?) in the right hand, lower section of the photograph.

Did you Hear That?

Unfortunately for some, the risk was very real. It's been said that a young couple was parked there years ago, steaming up the car windows (as young couples are known to do), when they heard strange sounds, almost as if some creature was scratching their car.

The young (amorous) man, likely wanting to impress his date, popped out of the car to bravely check the situation out and supposedly told his girl that he'd be right back.

The next thing his date knew, she was being roused awake the next morning by the local cops. They asked her to exit the car and told her, whatever she did, not to look back. She said she wouldn't look back, but instinctively spun around when she realized she'd left her purse in the vehicle. To her utter horror she oh-so-clearly saw why she had been told not to look. Her murdered boyfriend's body, punched full of bloody holes, was lying splayed out on top of the car roof.

A Frightful Death

Another rumor going around is that a famous politician that lived on the road died of fright looking out his window into the back woods. John Haussermann, a lawyer, politician, and gold miner was the person the rumor is centered around. He was a rollicking, jovial fellow, known as "The Gold King of the Philippines." According to accounts, Haussermann was extremely rich, yes, but also a generous and kind guy. Although this is not confirmed at all, the legend goes that Haussermann was staring out the window of his home toward the woods/fields and became so spooked, it took his breath away. For good.

Granted, this fellow was not a spring chicken when he left this early plain; in fact, he died in 1965 at the astoundingly ripe age of ninety-seven years. But, the rumor that his death was precipitated because he "saw" something/someone remains, and will not die. Such is the stuff of urban legends; and Pond's Run has got all of the components of a fantastic urban legend. And then some.

Another part of the legend has to do with a couple parked at Pond's Run Road who also heard the scratching sound outside their car. This couple, however, were well aware of what had happened to the other couple who'd once heard that sound, and they pealed out of the area immediately. Upon arriving home, the fellow got out to open the car door for his date (do people still do that anymore?) and he was shocked when his palm encompassed a hook that was stuck in the door handle.

To add fuel to the Pond's Run Hook Man fire, in the 1990s, people have reported being chased/followed by vehicles while on that road—namely a Greyhound Bus and a van. For one group, it occurred after the radio went nuts and the temperature dropped drastically inside their own vehicles. The most frightening aspect of those chases was that they could not see anyone in the driver's seat. That would be enough to keep the legend going well into the next millennium.

Filmmaker Shane Reinert and partner Andy Crosier paid a visit to Pond's Run with the film's narrator, Richard Crawford.

"We first went in the daytime," says Reinert with a grin. "It's been said that there were many murders here on this bridge in Pond's Run. The bridge was constructed of wood before, and several different witnesses have told me 'that [the bridge] looked like it was soaked in blood,'" he adds.

The bridge has since been replaced. Reinert went on to say that all the bigger houses in Pond's Run have lights pointing toward the woods at awkward angles. Why would they do that? he wonders. Why not have the lights stationed on the driveway or other areas that are used around the house?

"We came back that night to do a reenactment. It's so dark, there is no light anywhere," Reinert continues. "It's unbelievably dark. We were in this big grassy area, and we start walking [up toward the bridge] and we hear crashing in the woods." Reinert's voice quickened at the memory.

"It sounded like branches or a tree was falling down," he says, "so we figured let's hurry up and get this shot!" They did get the shot, but Reinert is quick to admit that he felt extremely uneasy out there in that wooded thrashing blackness. "It was difficult for me to be on that bridge," Reinert says. "We need to hurry up!" he told Crosier. "If the real hook man's here, he's gonna come up and kill me!"

As semi-humorous as the duo finds their fear to be later on, there's no denying that they heard something in the woods "and it was on two feet," says Reinert. "It was so deathly quiet, then, all of a sudden you hear crackling. Whatever it was, it sounded like it was heavy. It was an experience."

Another strange thing was that while they were out there, filming a scene by the Pond's Run turn off, Andy almost got hit, not once, but multiple times, by a car.

"Three times he almost got hurt," says Reinert. "The cars just seemed to come out of nowhere."

Whether you believe in the legend of the hook man or not, there's something mysterious about that stretch of road in New Richmond, Ohio. Something that you wouldn't want to come face to face with on a dark, moonless night—and maybe not even in the light of day.

Pond's Run Road is located off of County Road 52 in New Richmond, Clermont County, Ohio.

Chapter 17
The Promont House

The Promont House, located at 906 Main Street in Milford, Ohio, takes the word grandiose to a new level. The massive but eloquent white-painted structure is filled with historic grace and charm and, perhaps, a ghost or three. To be honest, there is some who claim it is haunted, while others claim it isn't. Whatever your take on things, the structure is as impressive from the inside as it is from the outside. This Italianate-style home was constructed during 1865 to 1867, and it was likely one of the most exclusive homes in the Cincinnati area.

Promont is a jaw-dropping vision that serves the public as a living history museum; and, perhaps some nice digs for some who are deceased. The museum offers an interesting and accurate view of Victorian life, from clothing and furnishings down to the most popular toys of the time. It also houses a gift shop, research library, educational opportunities, and the chance to have "afternoon tea, lunch, or brunch." Not to mention a vast array of photos, files, and other historical records.

Although Promont House offered several haunted tours with local historian, researcher, and author Richard Crawford in 2006, there are still signs that complete acceptance of the anomalies that might be present has not and, perhaps, never will occur.

Despite the uncertainty of some in society, strange, inexplicable things continue to happen, even in glorious manses. The Promont House has been around for well over one hundred years, and like it or not, has been the site of a tragic suicide, unexplained noises, strange "messes", and mysterious deaths.

The Promont House, Milford, Ohio.

A Haunted Bed

The structure was once the home of John M. Patterson, the Governor of Ohio. Patterson, who was believed to have been suffering from a difficult and deadly kidney disease, ended up breathing his last in his bedroom inside the walls of his home in 1906. It seems that ghosts do not need a whole building or land area in order to hang around, because Patterson's own deathbed seemed to serve the purpose just fine.

So much so, the bed was removed (years after his death) and put into another home in Batavia, Ohio. Odd noises, creaks and vibes from the bed were fairly constant in the bed's new home, however. Add in the fact that the bedding, despite being straightened to a tee, would be found rustled up and/or off-kilter moments later and you've got the makings of a nifty piece of haunted furniture. If the bedding were re-straightened; it would make no difference. It wouldn't be long before it would again be rustled up. Interesting, yes, but not ideal for achieving a peaceful night's sleep. Thus, the bed was eventually taken down and stored away.

Even though that bed is no longer at Promont, mysterious and sad things still occur. A woman committed suicide in the top of the tower of the structure. People who worked at the site were treated to a variety of unexplained noises and shuffling, and some employees listed specific areas of the home where they flat out refused to venture into.

According to Crawford, on the Dark Figure Productions Video: *True Ghost Stories from Ohio with Richard Crawford*, a nurse who worked there refused to go in the basement because he'd often hear sounds/movement there. Crawford added that there have also been workers that refuse to work anywhere at Promont by their lonesome, because they'd simply heard too much strange stuff prior.

Also on record is a lady who worked there after hours (as a librarian) who said she was there with another worker and they both heard someone climbing up the stairwell. Despite the fact that they knew they were the only ones in the place, they called out that Promont was closed. Undaunted, the footsteps continued onward and upward towards them. When the ladies rose and went to the stairs to confront the visitor, they found nobody there. They were understandably afraid and quickly did a one-eighty and exited out the back door via the second floor exit that night.

Those who are hired to clean the structure have said they've witnessed fresh tobacco stains on the floor they had just cleaned minutes earlier. The spirits are obviously not fond of spittoons.

The last night Crawford had given a tour there, they were inside Governor Patterson's room (about thirty were present). Crawford got a chill "as if somebody was putting a hand down my shirt." As they were talking several people felt a cold spot go by them, as if something or somebody was slipping between them. Then the bed "very slightly gives way as if somebody was laying in it," noted Crawford. It was at that point that everybody decided that they'd seen enough.

If you're interested in seeing history in action, The Promont House is located at 906 Main Street in Milford, Ohio.

Chapter 18
Lonely Rebecca

Rebecca McClung's memory lingers throughout Mason, Ohio, long after her untimely murder over 100 years ago. Tea Roses Tea Room and Gift Shop, owned and operated by Sally Gasior, is located in the building where the murder occurred, but from its warm, inviting atmosphere, believe me, if you were just stopping by, you'd never know it. The fact that Rebecca's presence is still felt roaming the site (especially upstairs) to this day could be because her death is labeled as the only unsolved murder case in that cozy quiet town, or it could be because Rebecca has never really left the premises. If there's one thing for certain when it comes to Rebecca McClung, it is that time does not heal all wounds. For although her murder is officially labeled as unsolved, most people familiar with the case are quite certain they know who did it: her own husband, John.

In Rebecca's case, a century of lying entombed right next to your killer (also known as the man you'd pledged marital vows to) is like pouring salt in the wound of a tattered soul. To be buried beside him was likely the final affront to this poor woman, who was defenseless against the man determined to pummel away her life.

When Rebecca Dawson married John McClung, he was fifteen years her senior. It is assumed that she loved him and that she never could have known that this fellow would attack her viciously and get off scot-free after doing so—an act that was shocking to everyone around town back then, and still is, today.

Tea Roses Tea Room and Gift Shop in Mason, Ohio.

So shocking that it could be the reason that there has been so much paranormal "action" at what used to be "The Old Hotel," on Main Street in Mason, Ohio, ever since. Things are moved around, windows are opened and closed, visions of a woman in black are witnessed floating upstairs. Such instances are commonly attributed to the one and lonely, Rebecca.

The Main Street brick building has been the backdrop for numerous roles in the town's history. It was initially erected at the bequest of John McClung. A new home was built to his specifications, and in 1888, John and his wife, Rebecca, moved in and lived there right up until her horrific murder on April 12, 1901.

In the April 17, 1901, edition of the *Miami Gazette*, news of Rebecca's murder was published, along with a brief background of the McClungs. The Gazette stated that the McClungs had sold their home six months prior to her murder but opted to stay there afterwards and were renting.

Hidden Away

Almost unbelievably, it was also reported that Rebecca McClung never left this residence (prison?) in the thirty-plus years they had called the building home. Ever. Even more amazing was the fact that in spite of this, Rebecca knew the names and faces of every single townsperson in Mason.

"She would sit by the hour and look through her shutters at the passersby," the *Gazette* reports. It was also reported that Mr. McClung was, by nature, a loner, as well.

"While business interests, of course, forced Mr. McClung somewhat more into touch with the public, he was almost as much of a recluse as his wife," the paper says.

Given this information to stew upon, one can't help but wonder: Was Rebecca McClung a recluse by her choice—or was it her husband's choice for her? The fact that she was considered to be quite beautiful and would sit upstairs, incessantly staring out that second-story window at the vibrancy of the world strolling by gives pause for thought. Was she like a bird trapped within a cage, longing to escape the confines of house walls? Alternatively, was she there of her own will?

What had caused John McClung to suddenly and violently lose his temper at his wife, to the extent of demolishing her face? Nobody knows, and even sadder, nobody will likely ever know.

According to the *Gazette*, "Mr. McClung disclaimed all knowledge of the crime. His testimony really being that if he had committed it, he did not know it. One noticeable fact of the inquest was that he did not really deny the crime." One newspaper account stated that John McClung "got off" by a claim of insanity.

"Although his clothing, trousers, and hands were covered in blood and bloody footsteps were found all throughout the house, he was found not guilty," reported the *Pulse-Journal* of Mason, Ohio.

The *Gazette* reported that Mrs. Sallie Baymore and Mr. Dill, who John had sold the house to, testified that they heard what seemed to be John McClung's footsteps rapidly descending the stairs following "four bloodcurdling screams," coming from Rebecca's dying lips.

Rebecca was beaten to death with wood from the very fireplace she so often sat beside. According to newspaper accounts of that time, every single bone in this lovely woman's head was crushed. She was sixty; her husband was seventy-five.

In the wake of her murder, the Mason place ultimately evolved from a private home to a hotel to a boarding house (half-a-buck a day would get you a room back then). The boarding house ceased operation in 1966.

The building was then again a private residence, and after that a cozy antique shop was operated from part of the site, as well. The structure has had more than one life in the sense that a tornado, in 1974, roared through Mason and took the roof with it. The roof was restored, rather than condemned, and the historic building was then revamped and opened as a gift shop. After the gift shop ceased to operate there, several lawyers took residence inside for a brief time, and then a fancy, eclectic restaurant operated from the site for several years.

Tea Time

In 2006, Gasior, a Mason resident since 1993, gave the building a new purpose and the town a new treasure by opening Tea Roses Tea Room and Gift Shop. If you're in Mason, stop by and try some of their delectable scones and choose from a selection of thirty-two teas to go with them. Lunch is available, too, and their tomato basil soup and strawberry chicken salad are hands-down customer favorites. Moreover, who knows? You might also get a glimpse of the woman in black if you're very, very lucky.

Gasior is well versed in the life and death of the woman that lived and died on the site so many years before her. "Rebecca's buried next to John, but John was a suspect in her murder, and it's considered the only unsolved (murder) mystery in Mason to this day, because although he was put on trial, he wasn't convicted. So technically, the murder was never solved, although there really weren't any other suspects," says Gasior.

This is where Rebecca would sit and watch the world stroll by below her. It's also the room where she was murdered.

"There were no signs that the house was broken into," Gasior continues. "Rebecca was found at two-thirty in the morning by a seamstress that lived in the house with them, and John came back in and said that he'd been in the barn at two-thirty in the morning, and that the blood on his hands wasn't her blood—instead, that it was his dry, cracked skin," says Gasior. "John blamed (her death) on people doing some work outside. [The town dump used to be right across the road.] After his trial John required hospitalization for his heart condition and he died in 1904 from heart failure."

"This is where they found her," says Gasior, pointing to an area in front of the fireplace. In the light of a glorious spring morning with the sun streaming through the windows, it's hard to fathom that a woman once lay upon the wooden floor in a pool of her own blood, much less that she was most likely put there by a man whom she supposedly once loved.

"John was a grouchy old man that didn't like kids," says Gasior. "They had no kids." It doesn't sound like a fairy tale life in the least. Perhaps that's why Rebecca has chosen to reappear periodically after her death.

"Most of the people's stories are not of seeing Rebecca, but of things that you just can't explain," says Gasior. "We say sometimes you give [Rebecca] the credit or the blame; doesn't matter what happens."

Before Gasior set up shop, she shared that there "was a lawyer that tried to do some remodeling. They tell stories about hearing doors slamming AFTER they'd taken them all down [for remodeling purposes]."

A previous owner who had been there for a dozen years stopped by for lunch and reluctantly shared that although "I don't believe in those things, I did see Rebecca one time. When I closed one night, I saw her on the steps—she was standing at the top of the [second floor] steps. All those years, people kept asking questions [about Rebecca]; we were kind of sick of it," she adds with a grin. "[Rebecca] was about my size; dressed in black with a pulled-in waist, and a long skirt, all black. Well, she just stood there and I said, 'Oh!' It caught me so unaware," the former business owner claims, "and then she was gone."

The previous owner also recalled a particular woman [customer] who refused to come into the shop. Instead, she had the staff fetch the items she desired for her. Others who would come into the shop may have "felt" a presence. Finally this former owner said out loud, "'Rebecca, just play and have a good time.'"

For several years the building was used as a restaurant called the Chokolate Morel, says Gasior. During this time a woman had come to the culinary establishment specifically to make contact with Rebecca. Throughout her meal the woman was "talking" to Rebecca, asking her to make herself known to her. Unfortunately, the woman neither heard nor saw anything from the woman from beyond. Disappointed by the lack of contact, but her faith in Rebecca's presence still in tact, Gasior says that before leaving, the woman asked a favor of the resident spirit.

"I'm going to the casino, so give me good luck [since you didn't show yourself to me]." According to Gasior, the lucky woman was rewarded for efforts. She won $8,000 at the casino that night.

Gasior discovered Rebecca's presence herself. "Before we were opened, we had had some work in the basement and we were leaving the windows open to air it out—like on a Friday," Gasior shares. "Before I left, I closed up all the windows in the basement because it was going to rain and nobody was here over the weekend. This was during pre-opening days. I came back in on Monday and the basement windows were open. Two of them! It's like 'I know I locked the door to the basement and closed those windows!'"

There have been other instances as well. "We had a little Christmas tree on the mantle, and the servers came up one morning and the tree was under the table. I don't know why [Rebecca moved it]," Gasior says.

The shop owner went on to share that a fellow that worked at the cemetery had an astounding experience of actually seeing Rebecca—clear as day. "He was in the office working and heard someone come in, says Gasior. He swiveled around to see this woman, dressed 'real old-fashioned' standing there. She asked the fellow where Rebecca McClung was buried. He said something like, 'Well, let me look it up,' and he turned around to check the records. When he turned back to tell her the grave's location, he saw that the woman was gone.

"Later on, he was at the historical society," notes Gasior, "and he saw a picture and said, 'Who is that woman? That's the lady that came in and asked about Rebecca.' The man was told by the surprised volunteer that the woman in the picture was Rebecca McClung; and that she had been dead for 100 years."

Employees of the tea room have also had their own encounters with Rebecca. "Linda [who works in the kitchen] thought she saw someone go down the hallway and thought it was someone else working; then realized that there's nobody else working up here," says Gasior.

"Two of the other servers were up in Rebecca's room cleaning up one day, and one of them felt something fall out of her pocket and saw a ball of yarn roll across the floor. She looked at the other server and said, 'Did you see that?' The other server said, 'Yes,' and they looked back again. The ball of yarn was gone. The server said 'Okay, Rebecca,' and then a chair fell over," adds Gasior. The two ladies quickly fled the room.

It seems Rebecca is not the only being that still hangs around the Main Street structure. "There's a woman that lived in the house years ago, and she still doesn't like to go in the Rose Room because that's where she and her sister slept," says Gasior. "They would see a figure in the window that wasn't Rebecca."

Christmastime is not only active for Gasior and her employees and their patrons, but for Rebecca as well. It seems like the holiday season gets Rebecca all revved up and ready to play—whether it be by transferring the miniature Christmas tree from the fireplace mantel to a spot under a table or by moving the little "presents" around the place.

Autumn seems to be another active "Rebecca" time, says Gasior, adding that, ironically, she did not notice anything at all on the anniversary of Rebecca's death.

The Anomaly Response Network (ARN) ghost hunting group came to Tea Roses around Halloween, 2006. During the ghost hunting process, Gasior had a tea party underway for the occasion, which seemed to hamper the ARN investigation somewhat, admitted Sean Feeney, the ARN founder and director. A typical investigation is usually held without outside visitors/interference, to try and draw out the ghost and so the data can be interpreted without question of other human involvement. The investigation was chronicled in *The Cincinnati Enquirer*, which also somewhat dictated the format, recalls Feeney. Although they found nothing concrete using their specialized instruments, it seems Rebecca has a sense of humor and found her own way to play a little Halloween trick.

While the investigators were in another location, one of the decorative pumpkins that was on the mantel flipped up and flew smack dab in a patron's lap; this being quite a feat since the woman was sitting four feet away. Their cameras had not been set up in the room where the tea party was held; the ghost hunters, thinking it would be the last place that Rebecca would surface. Chalk one up for Rebecca!

Feeney indicated that they would like to revisit the site and perform an investigation when there was less action going on. He believes there certainly could be something there.

Gasior takes the likelihood of an additional guest (or two) at her establishment in stride. "I can't figure out what there would be to be afraid of," she says. "Rebecca was the one that might not be happy buried next to John and might prefer to be here instead."

Gasior smiles. "Oh, she's around."

Tea Roses Tea Room and Gift Shop is located at 101 E. Main Street in Mason, Ohio. Web site address: www.tearoses.net.

Chapter 19
Sweet Lips

Sometimes cemeteries hold secrets that even the headstones don't reveal. The Smyrna Cemetery on Smyrna Road in Felicity, Ohio, in Clermont County is such a place. There is one particular monument that shimmers atop not only the person whose name is engraved on it, but someone else who is supposedly buried beneath there, as well.

"Smyrna Cemetery is located at the end of a little dead-end road in Felicity, which is a very small place to begin with," says filmmaker, Shane Reinert. "There is a gravestone there that is supposed to glow or be a little bit brighter." The area was the site of a Shawnee Village. "Sweet Lips was a Shawnee Sorceress who was leading her people [in Felicity]," says Reinert.

By the 1780s, white folk were coming down the Ohio River and wreaking havoc on the Indians. This area was known as the Miami slaughterhouse because of the many deaths on both sides during this time.

Sweet Lips was responsible for instigating the attack of a group of surveyors on Christmas Eve night, 1787. No one was killed, but several men were hurt and one man was taken hostage—a fellow named Peter Hastings.

According to Reinert, upon his capture, the tribe striped him naked and painted him black, "which means," shares Reinert, "'you're condemned and we're going to kill you.'"

For whatever reason, Sweet Lips' heart overran her tribe's wishes, because she took a liking to this particular white man. Turns out the feeling was mutual (at least made to seem so by Hastings). Sweet Lips was so taken with this white man, she allowed him to escape the fate of death one night. Before she released him, however, she told him that the only way she'd let him go was if he promised to come back and see her again.

It's also believed that Sweet Lips sweetened the pot, so to speak, by promising that when Hastings returned, he would receive some land, which was Hastings' goal in the first place.

"So a couple of years goes by," says Reinert, "and the white man comes back, saying, 'I'm here to get my land.' It was September of 1795 when Hastings arrived back at Smyrna Village. He boldly informed the tribe that he had come back to get what he was promised by their leader. Hastings' demands were made after the signing of the Greeneville Treaty (which made the Native Americans give up their land). The tribe was already extremely agitated because they had already lost much of their land in the years prior and the fact that they would now have to surrender even further tracts, raised their hostility levels toward their leader to the breaking point.

"The braves were furious," says Reinert. "They didn't know anything about this promise of land and they chased Peter Hastings away." Not content to leave it at that, they went after the Shawnee sorceress with a murderous vengeance.

Exactly how she was murdered is not completely certain. One scenario is that her own tribe at the Smyrna Cemetery site burned her at the stake. Others claim that the Shawnee made Sweet Lips dig her own grave, and while she was praying over it, they threw a tomahawk at her. It struck her in the head and her body tumbled within the grave she'd dug.

Reinert goes on to say that the Methodists started a church on the site in the 1800s, and they initiated a cemetery there. More than one member of the congregation noticed a woman who was in a foggy form in the cemetery at night. It became more and more commonplace to see this vision. Member after member would remark on this strange woman's presence, and it became so commonplace, that the church eventually moved because of it.

There is no complete certainty of where in that cemetery Sweet Lips is buried, but it is widely believed that she lies beneath a particular gravestone that gleams extra bright at night. A portion of the stone has been checked by scientists and is no different than the other stones around it. There is no scientific explanation for this.

"There is someone buried on top of [Sweet Lips]," says Reinert. "There have been reports of heavy mists and fog down there when there's no reason for it. Many people were seeing an Indian woman walking through the graveyard next to the church," says Reinert. "One of the neighbors of the cemetery said he'd have fog come up under his garage door and fill his whole garage. Very strange."

What is also strange is that when Andy Crosier was taking still photos of the narrator/Clermont County historian and tour guide, Richard Crawford, in the Smyrna Cemetery, one of the photos showed a bright stream of light next to Crawford—a stream of light that was not visible at all when taking the photo. To further "strange" things up, the stream of light is missing its center component. There is a top and a bottom to the light, but no center. Crosier was amazed and very pleased. So pleased, that it was the photo used for the jacket of their DVD release. Could that be Sweet Lips "posing" for the DVD?

This photo of historian, researcher, and narrator Richard Crawford, was taken while he was at the gravesite of Sweet Lips. *Photo courtesy of Dark Figure Productions filmmaker Andy Crosier.*

Southgate House in Newport, Kentucky.

Chapter 20
The Southgate House

The Southgate House in Newport, Kentucky, looms majestically atop a hill, its veranda offering a panoramic view of the crowds that visit the bustling Newport area. Shops, bookstores, taverns, restaurants, the Newport Aquarium— pretty much you name it—are all within walking distance of this historic building, which is now a "happening" music and art venue. It's a bar with a fun and varied history where you can stop in, hear some cool tunes, and sip a cold one. Of course, it's haunted (why else would it be in here?).

This mansion on Third Street has undergone numerous transitions throughout its almost 200-year existence, but has somehow always retained a whiff of regality. Local lawyer, Richard Southgate, built the structure in 1814, after his family had resided in a log cabin on the site for twenty-some years. The attorney eventually became a state representative and senator, as well a manufacturer of silk, and his prominence and opulence was reflected in his surroundings.

Southgate was huge; it originally occupied a full city block. It was a well-known building and vastly admired as being one of the first of Newport's truly grand homes.

Not surprisingly there is much history (haunted and otherwise) associated with the house, which has welcomed many prestigious guests, some of which are rumored to have not truly left.

In addition to a host of other dignitaries, the one and only Abraham Lincoln visited Richard Southgate at his home before he became the president of the United States, and the inventor of what's known as the Tommy Gun, Brigadier General John Tariaferro Thompson was born inside the house in 1860. The second Kentucky chapter of the Daughters of the American Revolution was born there, as well. It is also known that the Southgate House played host on December 30, 1835, to a large company of Captain Sherman's men. A great night was had by all (thanks to Southgate's generous hospitality) and fortified with great memories (and, perhaps, more than a few hangovers); the group departed the next day to fight for Texas' independence, and did so grandly. It is said the group played an important role in the Battle of San Jacinto.

Southgate's most recent purpose is as a prominent bar and music venue for the Northern Kentucky/Cincinnati area. It is a welcoming arena for both talented upcoming musicians as well as more established bands, and has been labeled by local press as "one of the best places to hear live music for its intimate setting and cozy sound."

The first floor, also known as Junie's Lounge, affords visitors an opportunity to sink the eight ball to the tunes of the landmark jukebox. The Ballroom, which is located downstairs, features a bar and balcony for larger performances. There is also a parlor on the second floor where more intimate and personal gigs take place. The newly renovated third floor art gallery hosts some of the best local, regional, national, and international art. If the stories and rumors are true, the other side has visited all floors of this grand mansion.

Southgate has a unique vibe that most assuredly transcends guitars and drums; things are seen and sounds are heard within the establishment that are often difficult to explain as coming from this earthly plain.

A good example of such comes from a longtime female employee of Southgate who recalls a yuletide experience that occurred a decade ago. The experience was pretty much out of this world.

"I have never seen ghosts," the employee makes it clear up front. "It's just that weird things happen. You hear noises...I'd always chalked it up to it being an old building."

Chalked it up to a creaky old building until Christmastime rolled around, however. "We had a guy that worked here and he always put the Christmas tree in between the French doors," the employee shares. "Well, one night—I think it was on a Friday night—I'm on the end of the bar, there, waiting to finish the order, and the Christmas tree just went *schoop* [slid three or four feet] right into the corner. [Nobody was there.] Nothing fell off of it and I thought, 'Aw, I'm seeing things. That didn't just happen. I gotta quit drinking.'" The employee chuckles at the memory.

"I stood there, dumbfounded. I mean, what the heck is that about, right? The guy that put it up tended bar here and he was downstairs working the ballroom. He came up to get something and I told him, 'go look at the Christmas tree.'"

"Who the hell put it in the dang corner?" he demanded to know. The female bartender said "You're never gonna believe this one," and she relayed what she had just seen. The fact that the festive tree had been nigh on bursting with ornaments and decorations and none of them were as much as even tousled, did not go unnoticed by either of them. "He *had* to believe me. I couldn't have lifted it up," the bartender noted. "Blink your eye and you'd miss it."

That is not the only strange thing that has happened within Southgate's walls. Another fairly common occurrence has to do with the front door—which has a tendency to open and close by itself.

Many of the regular employees believe that the door opening "person" behind this anomaly is named Elizabeth. The female bartender expounds: "There is a woman named Elizabeth whose husband worked on the river boats; he went to Louisville every morning and came back late in the afternoon. Elizabeth would go up in the widow's peak so she could see his boat come in. Well, one day, his boat blew up and she saw it happen [ironic where she witnessed it from, isn't it?] and hung herself right up there in the widow's peak."

What is even more tragic is that her death was all for naught. "The fellow wasn't even on the boat," says the bartender with a shake of her head. "And I heard he came back the next day. Now when that door opens at night and closes by itself, we always say that's just Elizabeth going for a walk."

The bartender recalls another particularly memorable experience with a deep, smoker's chuckle. One night the door opened and nobody came in. [Several people witnessed this]," she says, "but there was one guy in here that night that was just going crazy [wondering how that could have possibly happened]." His complete shock and disbelief was amusing to those around him. Almost as amusing as Elizabeth's antics.

"I said to the fellow, 'Sit there a while, she'll be back in a half an hour. Well, he sat there and that door opened and nobody came in, and I mean, he lost it. He [screamed] 'Aaaaah!' You couldn't even see anybody," adds the bartender.

Brad Rubin, a local resident and founder of Paranormal Worlds recalls visiting the bar a while back. He was sitting there talking to his girlfriend when his beer slid all the way across the table and flipped right into his lap. "Did you see that?" he asked his girlfriend. Yep, Rubin says, she had, adding that nobody had bumped the table, either.

Despite such interesting and strange occurrences, it never truly seemed to frighten the employees. "I used to be in here by myself a lot at night and I never was really scared," says the female bartender. "Even if you hear mumbling or things like that, you just chalked it up. I'm not a believer in ghosts," she says. "If something weird happens, I think, what the heck… if it happens, hey, it happens," she adds with a shrug.

"Let's say the piano upstairs suddenly starts playing, although there is no one else in the building except for you," says the bartender. This has actually occurred several times. "If it happens, it happens!" she repeats with a grin.

Suzanne, another bartender, said she's been alone at Southgate House and heard somebody laughing. Oh, and sometimes there is knocking on the wall. Lots of knocking on the wall.

"Is somebody trying to get out of the wall?" Suzanne says, laughing and adding, "This is a very interesting building; a very nice place to work."

According to the history of the place and the stories that have been passed down over the years, it looks as if there might be three ghosts. The female one, already mentioned, who is named Elizabeth, the spirit of a little boy, and also one of a gentleman wearing a confederate uniform.

"Some guy told me he came in one day and he was in the john for a long time," recalls the longtime bartender, "and when he came out, they asked him what he was doing in there, and he said he was 'talking to some guy in a Confederate uniform.' She's also witnessed a patron who was standing at the stairwell landing, talking to somebody up at the top of the steps. "Who are you talking to?" she asked him. The fellow replied, "That guy up there." The bartender walked over to join him. "There IS no guy up there," she says. "That section of the building is closed."

Whatever might be seen or heard at Southgate is taken in stride by most who work there. After all, a building with so much history is bound to have some unusual patrons, some of them more intriguing than others.

Southgate House is located at 24 E 3rd Street in Newport, Kentucky. Web site address: http://www.southgatehouse.com/.

Chapter 21
Are You Looking at Me?
Spring Grove Cemetery

S pring Grove Cemetery and Arboretum is a gloriously green and expansive site for the living (and, perhaps, the dearly departed) to roam around in. There have definitely been some stories of ghostly encounters and strange vibes within this stunning arena, which is also the second largest cemetery in America. However, they seem relatively few, given its enormous expanse. This cemetery is a National Historic Landmark, worth a visit whether ghost hunting, nature loving, or both.

Spring Grove is housed in the City of Cincinnati, Hamilton County, Ohio. It came to fruition in the mid-1800s as a result of morbid necessity; the cholera outbreak of the 1830s and 40s was taking many lives and other graveyards were becoming full quickly. Spring Grove was the answer for the present, as well as the far and distant future.

Years ago, horse and buggy were the norm mode of transportation in this panoramic location and the charm of yesteryear still resonates. It's hard to believe how long some of the mausoleums have stood. There is an amazing abundance of the coffin-holding structures; they are proud, fancy, and ornate, some nestled within hillsides others perched on the banks of glistening ponds.

The fact that graves are buried within such jaw-droppingly gorgeous scenery almost makes it seem as if it should be immune to any potential hauntings. The monuments and statues bursting toward the sky in this 733-acre cemetery/arboretum and park make it feel more like a sublime residence than a sublime final resting place.

There is an explosion of color in spring, summer, and fall, as the blooming trees, flowers, and greenery rustle in the breeze. There are also lakes, ponds, bridges, and towering trees. It can feel nigh on romantic and enticing to stroll through the vast grounds. There is so much history, so much flora and fauna…so many famous dead.

Multitudes of important historical and war-time figures are buried at Spring Grove with over thirty Civil War generals and loads of important passed-away politicians too, including Salmon P. Chase, who was an Ohio senator, governor, and treasurer under Lincoln.

A sublimely spooky area in the amazing Spring Grove acreage is the Dexter Memorial. You will come upon this looming structure fairly quickly upon entering the Spring Grove grounds. It is the type of memorial that could be the perfect backdrop for a horror movie; but a comforting burial service for a loved one? Not so much.

The Dexter Memorial, Spring Grove Cemetery.

The gothic memorial screams "I'm haunted," and can impart the shivers, even on a warm, sunny day. You see the area where the coffins enter the structure, and the double-sided stairs that lead mourners up to the chapel doors.

Supposedly, if you sit on one of the front porches and look out over the grounds, you will be treated to a vision of two brilliantly white, shining dogs striding past the grand structure. The shimmering beasts just might stop and look at you if you're lucky.

Reports of other strange occurrences have filtered out over the years, many of them centered on a particularly realistic-looking grave marker. If you visit Spring Grove, make it a point to navigate up to Lot 100. There you will see a bust of a man's head (and, perhaps, it might see you). Actually, it looks innocuous enough until you venture closer; no, even closer(!), and take a moment to gaze into the bust's eyes.

"Are you looking at me?" you might find yourself thinking, because those vibrant orbs sure seem like they could be doing just that. Rumor has it that the eyes are human, but of course that isn't possible. They would have rotted out long ago. Instead, they are actually glass—the most realistic-looking human glass eyes you're likely to ever encounter.

My son peering inside the Dexter Memorial; and it looks like he's not alone!

As if that isn't enough to twirl your stomach, it is rumored that the bust on Lot 100 will actually rotate its head in order to keep those orbs centered on passersby. Just in case, when you visit the lot, be polite and make sure you wave...and smile.

There are other instances of paranormal encounters at Spring Grove. It was written on The Forgotten Ohio web site that a groundskeeper there 'fessed up that once, while he was mowing, he "thought he saw hands poking out of the ground." Whoa, that would be enough to put some zip in one's step. The fellow likely completed his lawn work in record time that day.

Make sure that you visit during the proper hours and respect the dead, *and* the living visiting their passed-on loved ones. Follow the rules. Not only because it's the right thing to do, but because it's been noted that individuals that disrespect the grounds and gravestones at Spring Grove are followed with years of bad luck. Nobody wants that.

When you do visit, while strolling through the site, you might find yourself thinking, "Whoa, I could live here!" Then when it hits you that only the dead "live" there, you quickly retract the thought. But hey, since we all must go sometime, this place would seem to be the ultimate final address.

Spring Grove Cemetery is located at 4521 Spring Grove Avenue in Cincinnati, Ohio (Hamilton County).

The eyes of this bust in Spring Grove appear to be real; and really following you.

Chapter 22
Grandma's Never Really Left

There is a charming two-story house with a welcoming front porch in the heart of Maysville that is filled with years of family memories and, it seems, a ghost or two, as well. Anne Henderson and her husband, Keith, now live in what was once her grandmother's house. Actually, Anne has lived in the house, on and off, for much of her life. When she was younger, she lived with her grandmother there, and although it was a happy time, she admits that she always "felt" like she wasn't alone upstairs.

From her earliest recollections, Anne can recall having a strange feeling atop that landing. Her room was on the second floor at the top of the stairs, she says, but it wasn't the bedroom itself that bothered her. It was that open space outside it.

She never liked her bedroom door to be open "because I always felt like there was something in the hallway," she says. "It felt like someone or something was watching me." Anne adds that her grandmother wanted her to have her bedroom open so she could hear her if need be, but Anne would wait until "grandma" went to sleep and then leap up and shut her bedroom door.

"I didn't know what it was," Anne admits, "but I just didn't like the feeling." Even when she had to go to the bathroom, she would run from her room into the bathroom and quickly shut the door behind her. To this day, she still feels like there's a presence of some kind up there, but it doesn't bother her nearly as much as it did when she was a child. "It's just something that is there," she says matter-of-factly.

Anne's life has come full-circle, from marrying and having children, to divorce, to a second marriage to Keith; and, ultimately, the couple moving into Anne's childhood home.

Keith, who never met Anne's grandmother, has had plenty of his own paranormal experiences in the house. It started about a year after they moved in. Keith recalls that he saw two shadowy figures in the corner. According to Keith, one of them looked like a black lady and one looked like a white lady.

"I asked Anne, 'Did your grandmother ever have a black lady stay with her?'" They came to find out that there was an African American lady that used to come from California and stay with Anne's grandmother during the summertime months.

Keith recalls another incident very well. "This was the one that scared me," he admits, wearing a wide grin. "It was about four o'clock in the morning, I was asleep upstairs and felt this cat swiping on my leg about four or five times."

"I walked past him and he shot up out of bed," says Anne. "I said, 'What is the matter with you? And Keith said, 'Something just touched my leg.'" Their cat was in another room at the time.

Keith is one of those people that is intuitively psychic. He has no idea when thoughts will come to him or what he will say, for that matter. "It just comes out of my mouth," he says. Keith has predicted where friends will meet their future marriage partners and says that his whole family, on his mother's side, has the same gift.

"My mother predicted the earthquake that was coming," relays Keith. "She had dreams of it a month before it happened and we used to laugh at her. She told us the street was splitting."

How could there be an earthquake there? It wasn't San Francisco, for heavens sake, it was Kentucky.

Well, there *was* an earthquake in Maysville, Kentucky, in 1981. "I was up on the hillside picking blackberries when it hit," says Keith. "I was hanging onto a tree thinking, 'Well, I guess my mother was right,'" he recalls with a laugh. They said the quake was one of the largest spanning; it went all the way from Lake Erie to somewhere in Missouri.

My grandmother predicted who my cousin would marry about five years before she married him, says Keith. Given his family prowess for psychic intuitiveness, it's not too surprising that Keith has heard and seen a wide variety of paranormal activity in the house. Nothing that would make him feel the urge to move, however. Anne agrees.

"I've heard walking across the floor upstairs, and I've heard doors opening and closing upstairs when you're the only person in the house. You get used to it," says Anne. Her son, Nathan Wells (a co-founder of PINK), has had his own experiences, too. He's heard male voices talking downstairs, when nobody else was there.

"The one experience that stays in my mind more than anything was when Keith and I were moving back in here," says Anne. "The house was completely empty, furniture-wise. Myself, Keith, my brother, and the boys were here. We were talking about our childhood and Grandma, and all of the sudden we hear this noise upstairs, and we all ran upstairs to see what it was. Of course, there is nothing upstairs. My brother goes into the bathroom and we see that the people who had moved out had left one shower ring. The perplexed family members ultimately deduced that the sound they'd heard was the shower ring being twirled around. They strongly believe "Grandma" made it happen to acknowledge their presence and welcome them home.

It is not just their grandmother that is hanging around the house, however. One night, Anne woke up and saw shadowy, male, hooded figures encircling her bed. According to the Maysville resident, they looked like a version of the Grim Reaper. "It was like a coven surrounding my bed. I knew they were looking at me," she says. Her response was not what one would typically expect, however. She simply just rolled over.

How was she able to do this? "I know evil is not going to touch me, so I'm okay," says Anne, flashing a warm smile.

The Maysville couple is both grounded and open to what they see as part of the world around them. They view ghosts as simply a component of life.

Keith and Anne consented to the Paranormal Investigation of Northern Kentucky (PINK) ghost-hunting group to come in and do an investigation. Mike Palmer, the co-founder and lead investigator of the group, recalls that before they had even set up any equipment, the group and several members of the family (minus Anne and Keith) were sitting in the living room chatting. It was about eleven-thirty at night and while they were discussing family whereabouts, Palmer said that they heard a distinct female voice from upstairs call out, loud and clear: "Anne?"

Turns out, there was nobody upstairs (not of the human variety, at least) and Palmer says they came away with several documented EVPs from the Henderson house as well.

Anne and Keith were not surprised. After all, they've been living with the voices, noises, and paranormal "company" for many years. When Keith senses them to be around, he just says things like, "Hi, Grandma, or whatever," he shares with a grin.

"I'm glad to be able to talk freely about a subject that most people would look at you like you've grown two horns and a tail," says Anne. "It is so refreshing, and I'm so glad that more of the paranormal and spiritual aspect of life is being brought to the forefront in addition to the religious aspect. Because I feel we are spiritual beings having an earthly experience, not earthly beings having a spiritual, experience, which seems to be the consensus of the majority."

Chapter 23
The Stetson House

S outh Main Street in Waynesville, Ohio, is a Mecca for antique shoppers, history lovers, and ghost hunters. The sidewalks encourage visitors to stretch their legs and stroll through the charming town in search of a great deal. The history tours and paranormal happenings of the area implore those who stop by to also stretch their minds. So much unexplained activity has been documented and claimed in Waynesville that quite honestly it seems like anybody you ask in this place has had something occur to them personally and/or knows others—sometimes many others—who have.

Directly across the street from the Anderson Triple Axe Murder site, for example, is the Stetson House. This is a rather nondescript looking structure from the outside, but reports from the inside make it anything but boring and usual.

It's been said that mirrors won't stay put on the walls and the scent of gingerbread periodically infuses the air—perhaps lovingly mixed together in a kitchen that only stood long ago (for there is no kitchen there now). You can't help but wonder: Just who is baking this delectably smelling treat and, more importantly, how can I get a piece?

The house is known as the Stetson House because Louisa, the sister of the famed hat maker, John Stetson, once called it home. Waynesville historian Dennis Dalton shares that it was in 1865 that Louisa Stetson Larrick cut the marital ties and left her husband of twenty-seven years, Hiram Larrick, alone to tend the farm in rural Waynesville. She'd had it with rugged frontier life.

Her move back to town (to civility) and into the house on 234 South Main was a move toward independence. According to Dalton, she had married Hiram in 1838, and they lived on the frontier for years. She found frontier life "very rough and very distasteful." Town was much more her style, so she moved back and she stayed there until her death.

Twice during the years of 1861 to 1865, Louisa was visited by her gravely ill younger brother John Stetson. It's reported that John had gone west to try and regain his health, and he certainly had a lot of health to regain; he was tubercular and asthmatic. In fact, so much so, the doctor had told him he'd never survive.

During this time, John had been turned down for inclusion in the family hat-making business, so he opted to trek to Ohio to make his fortune while getting his strength back. He stayed with Louisa during the summer of 1861, and also during this time, took up with some wild gold miners.

Ever the natural entrepreneur, John then traveled further west where he incurred a small fortune in panning gold. Following that venture, the now famed Stetson entered into business partnerships with some brick makers in St. Joseph, Missouri, thinking that all of the pioneers would need building materials. Unfortunately, the company was flooded out of business as they were located right on the Missouri River.

Penniless now, says Dalton, John returned to Waynesville. During his trip back to Ohio, he created a hat for a freighter, which turned out to be a fine-looking specimen. So much so, John was paid a whopping five dollars in gold for his efforts.

"He told Louisa that if that man would pay him that much for a hat, maybe others would, too!" shares Dalton. "But John had no money," he adds.

At this time, John had completely regained his health, however, and was now capable of devoting himself both physically and intellectually to a new hat business. Louisa, "being the good woman that she was, believed in his dreams and schemes and she grubstaked him $60," says Dalton. Stetson then set out for Philadelphia, where he ultimately opened his one-man hat factory and built it all into a multimillion dollar hat empire. That first hat was the American Cowboy hat. Good to his word, he returned his sister's money in 1865.

The Stetson House on South Main Street in Waynesville, Ohio.

"Louisa was the one who believed in him," shares Dalton. "Well, he left her with a little legacy. Not gold and money, not stocks and bonds or anything like that." Unfortunately, his beloved sister Louisa ended up stricken with tuberculosis (also called the dreaded consumption) from her well-meaning brother.

Unlike her sibling's success in beating the wicked disease, Louisa was not so lucky. She ended up dying from its ravages in 1879, and her body is buried in Miami Cemetery just east of Waynesville.

"Since then, the house has been rather ordinary," says Dalton, "but in recent years, when antiques dealers bought the house and started bringing in their stock and renovating things, things began to happen. Mirrors would not stay on the wall, things on the walls would move back and forth."

Even those outside the structure noticed something was going on, shares Dalton. Not too long ago, for example, around Thanksgiving time, the then owner of the Stetson house was away to celebrate Thanksgiving with her family out of state. There was a little security light on behind the shop door and the man who was living across the street (coincidentally, smack dab in the house on the site where the triple axe murders took place) was having coffee and watching the eleven o'clock news, getting the weather report for his hunting excursion the next day.

According to Dalton, the gentlemen got up to fetch another cup of coffee and paused in front of the door to glance across the street. Upon doing so, he saw the figure of a small, dark-headed woman, her hair done up on her head. The fellow happened to mention to his wife, "You know, I think that's strange that Marge is up so awfully late working in her shop." His wife said, "Oh no, Marge is not there; she's out of state having Thanksgiving dinner with her family. It can't be her."

Dalton grins. "The man looked back across the street and said that the woman was wearing a high-collared dress that seemed to have long sleeves, and even with that door with those glass panes in it, he still couldn't see the bottom of her dress. She just stood there, staring out into the street, and right before his eyes she backed back into the lamplight and dissolved into the wall while he watched."

Who was this vision? Was it Louisa? Perhaps. There have been other strange things that have happened over the years as well, says Dalton. There was one particular instance, for example, that involved an eighteen-year-old clerk who was working at the shop on a Sunday, later afternoon. She was standing at the sales counter, that is just to the right of the front door, which she had just locked. The girl was continuing her duties to close up the place when there was a rattling at the front door.

The young woman leaned far over the counter and strained to see. All she could make out was an old-fashioned gloved hand on the outer doorknob. The glove was cuffed in wide lace and the girl assumed it was simply some little old lady who didn't realize she was closed.

"So the girl called out, 'I'm closed; could you come back tomorrow?'" says Dalton, "and there was this insistent rattling of the door again as the persistent person tried to get in. So the girl said, 'Oh, maybe you didn't hear me,' and she came around the counter and started toward the door, and as she did, she was saying, 'We're closed now,' only to find that there was no one there." Where had that little old lady gone so fast?

"It gave her a really strange feeling," says Dalton. Even so, she went ahead and finished her work for the evening. During the time all of this happened, her father was positioned out front at the curb in the car waiting to take her home.

"When she slid across the seat in the car," Dalton says, "the girl asked her father how long he'd been out there, and he replied oh, he'd been out there for a good while, waiting. 'Well who was the little old lady who came to the front door about ten minutes ago and kept rattling the front door?' she asked. Her father said, 'There was no one on the porch, no little old lady.' He'd been there for fifteen or twenty minutes and there hadn't been a living soul on that front porch," says a grinning Dalton.

Just who had rattled that door, donned in that old-fashioned lace-cuffed attire? Since the father of the worker saw nobody out on that front porch, it's more likely that the visitor to the shop was a lady from way down the block, perhaps as far as the Miami Cemetery, coming back for a visit.

Chapter 24
The Blue Room

"**I**t was the first time that I felt like I was home," says Claire May, of the large, two-story house in Maysville, Kentucky. "I guess because it was on family land."

"Home" was a house in the middle of a three-acre lot with a pond. "We had ducks and potbellied pigs and a cow," says Claire. "We loved it there." Claire was pregnant at the time with Jonathan. They already had three children in their blended family: Brittany, who was four, Kayla, who was ten, and Jonakkah, who was eleven, when they moved into the old house situated back on a rural road in 2002.

"The house belonged to my grandmother, and after she passed away, my aunt inherited it," says Claire. "They asked us if we wanted to come live there. We said, 'Okay!' she recalls with a hearty laugh.

Jon, who was a truck driver then, was planning on fixing up the place as time passed on, says Claire. The whole family was excited to be there. Not only was the house expansive, the acreage they had surrounding it was a child's dream.

What the family didn't know, however, was that somebody or thing was already living in a bedroom upstairs; in what was always called the blue room. The blue room had been known for its blue carpet and blue walls ever since her grandmother lived there. Seems things were so rosy when they first moved in that even her husband didn't notice anything awry with the blue room at first, which was not typical for this man.

"My husband has that little connection thing [psychic element] that I don't understand. He just *knows* if something's wrong and I don't have that. I really wish I did; then I would have known," says Claire.

The family did get the gist that something wasn't right about eight weeks into their stay. Claire was asleep in the master bedroom, which was downstairs in what was once the old parlor. Jon was gone on a truck run. The upstairs had three bedrooms with a room directly in the middle that was used as their playroom. Kayla, Jonakkah, and Brittany each had their own bedroom upstairs. Brittany's bedroom was the room to the left at the top of the stairs—the pretty blue room. All the kids were down for the night.

Brittany never watched scary movies or even mildly scary cartoons, and she was so very well grounded that she'd never even had a bad dream, says Claire. She'd go get her own water in the middle of the night and didn't ever use a nightlight, so it was a surprise when Claire awoke to the sounds of Brittany's screams.

"I want my mommy! Kayla, go get my mommy, go get my mommy, right now!" Claire heard her daughter yell. "She was literally screaming at the top of her lungs," says Claire, who raced up the stairs, and sure enough, her four year old was sitting in her bed, terrified. Claire figured that it was likely that her daughter had just experienced her first bad dream. They had only been in the new house for about two months, after all. She brought Brittany downstairs to sleep with her, and her older daughters were not unduly upset, they just padded back to their beds, relieved their sister's screaming had stopped. "I asked her if she'd had a bad dream and she said she thought she did, and it was no big deal," recalls Claire, "so I figured that was that."

That Wasn't *That*

The next night Brittany didn't have a problem being put to bed in her nice blue room. There were no pleas to sleep with mommy, no arguments, and no issues at all, says Claire, but her mother did notice that one of their dogs would not come into the room with them when she was tucking Brittany into bed. It had always come in before. This night the pooch waited at the threshold. Strange.

"I put Brittany in bed," says Claire, and about an hour after I went to sleep, I hear a thud and then I hear her scream again," she recalls.

"Kayla, get my mom. Get my mom! I want my mom!" Brittany yelled. Claire, again, raced back upstairs. "It's gettin' me, it's gettin' me! Get me out, get me out!" the child screeched out unceasingly to her mother. The strangest aspect of all of this was that Brittany would not get out of her bed, says Claire. She was hollering to her daughter to come to her as she raced up the stairs but Brittany would not budge from that mattress.

"I'm not going anywhere! Get me out of this room!" Brittany screeched. The bed was moved away from the wall and Claire assumed that Claire had been standing on the edge of the bed and jumping to make it move. She scooped her girl into her arms and the two went back downstairs to Claire's bed. Claire had told her husband about Brittany's "bad dream" via phone the night before while he was on the road, so he already knew that his daughter had endured a rough time.

That second night, Jon had come home very late, and having seen his wife and daughter sleeping in his bed, figured his little girl had had her second nightmare in as many days. He went upstairs to sack out in Brittany's room.

The Blue Room (Maysville, Kentucky). *Photo courtesy of Claire May.*

"I woke up at nine o' clock in the morning," says Claire, "and Jon's walking down the stairs with Brittany's bed in his hands.

"What are you doing?" Claire says she asked him. "She's sleeping in our room," Jon told his wife. "Nobody goes in that room again; she stays in our bedroom." Without asking why, Claire just nodded in agreement. She shared how talking about anything uncomfortable, especially ghosts, was just not done in her family. She came from a devoutly religious clan and things like ghosts were treated with the "drunk uncle" mentality. In other words, everybody knows that the uncle is perpetually imbibed, but nobody comes right out and says it. They all just pretend he's extra happy.

"So I go and get all of her clothes out of there," says Claire, "until there was nothing in that room. Period. I go up there that afternoon and start vacuuming and all of the sudden this bird flies across the room toward the window. It scared the crap out of me!" says Claire. "I'm trying to get this bird out, and I realize there's not any windows open. I have no idea how it got in there!"

Despite that odd fact, Claire reasoned that the winged visitor could be the root of the problem with the blue room. There must have been a bird in there the whole time; that's what was spooking everybody out. Her husband staunchly disagreed.

"There was no bird in here last night," he said. "Don't tell me there was a bird in there." Claire still believed that the bird must have been in the house, hiding out, and reasoned it was the cause of her daughter's panic.

This belief faded as the days passed, however, as Claire and her husband heard voices trailing down from the blue room several times—when nobody was in there.

"We don't do anything, don't say anything; we just all try to ignore it like it's not going on, the drunk uncle thing again," she quips. Two nights after Jon moved Brittany's bed to their room, the voices from what they knew was a completely empty blue room trickled down the stairs yet again. Clearly, voices. How long could they deny this?

"This is crazy, you guys," Claire told her family. "This is my grandma's house and she would not want us out of here! She told me about this house for years and they slept here often in the summertime." Claire insisted that her grandmother would have told her if something was wrong with the house. *Wouldn't she?* she wondered to herself.

Several days passed and Jon approached his wife. "Claire, I know I'm not home all the time and I'm not trying to scare you, but we need to move out of this house." She asked him why he would say such a thing. They were able to live in the home, save money, and had a great yard for their kids. "Then he showed me my daughter," says Claire, "and I see that she's got marks on her back. That was enough for me," she says. She told her husband, "We're done."

Still desperate to try and find a rational explanation for everything, Claire interrogated her oldest stepdaughter, asking if she was telling Brittany scary things or putting ideas into her head. Her oldest daughter was adamant that she'd done no such thing, "She just woke up screaming," she said, and having seen the sheer panic in her daughter's eyes, she believes her.

Trying to figure out exactly what was going on, Clair went to Brittany, asking her what really scared her in the blue room.

"Something was moving my bed and kept trying to come up and grab me," little Brittany told her mom. "What do you mean, *something*?" Claire asked. "I don't know!" Brittany told her mom, "But it was gonna get me if I touched the floor!"

"Did you see it in the daytime?" Claire asked. Brittany shook her head no. She told her mom that it was "only at night, and only after you went nigh-nigh." Later on, Brittany said that she had seen something alongside her bed. "I saw a hand," says Brittany. "It was a floating, bony hand [like an old man's hand]."

Kayla admits that when she looked inside the blue room, she would see strange shadows. The girl says that she was *compelled* to look in that room once dusk fell.

"Every night I'd have this feeling to look in and there'd be shadows on the ground. It was a shadow of a short person," she says. "One night, I was so scared I went and slept in my sister's bed."

Whatever was causing this chaos was not something that the Mays were willing to face. The family packed up all of their things and moved. An auction company took over the property to rent it for Claire's aunt.

It should be noted that Joe and Claire didn't tell anyone, certainly not her family, about what they'd experienced in the house. "My dad just knew we were moving; he didn't really know why, because he'd think I was lying and then *I* would be the drunk uncle," says Claire with a small chuckle. "We said we were moving because it didn't have central air conditioning, [Dad] didn't really buy that, but he didn't ask any questions."

Clueless as to what the family before him had experienced, a fellow rented the house and moved right in. About four weeks had passed when Claire's phone rang. "My Dad says, 'Was that house haunted?'" says Claire. "What? Why would you ask me a silly question like that, Dad?"

Her father told her that the guy that lived there called the auctioneer and said he woke up in the middle of the night in his bed knowing that he couldn't/shouldn't touch the ground. "He jumped from his bed out the door into the middle room," her father told Claire. The fellow told the auctioneer that he could "keep everything."

The house of the blue room. *Photo courtesy of Claire May.*

"'You've got to be kidding me," Claire replied. "What room was his room?" Her father told her that the fellow had slept in the blue room. He asked her why she wanted to know.

"I was just curious," Claire told her father. The father and daughter went to the house after the man had left and saw that "everything was exactly like it was when he went to bed," she says. "He really felt like something was gonna get him if he touched the floor [and he really left behind all of his possessions]."

"We started to move all his stuff out," says Claire, "and there was no way I was gonna move nothing out of the blue room." Instead, she gave her dad those duties. He went in there "and son of a gun," says Claire, "there was a bird in that room again. A black, purple sparrow-looking thing."

Her father thought the bird was coming in through the old shingles, but Jon had redone the roof and the chimney hole and shingles were covered up. Her father then deduced that the bird had come in when they were moving the other guy's stuff out. Just wanting to get it over with and get out of there, Claire agreed that the winged creature could have gotten inside the house that way, even though her gut told her otherwise.

Another couple moved in after that. They had a child. That family lasted about two weeks, says Claire. They not only left in a hurry, they, too, left without taking any of their belongings. They told the auction company that the house was haunted (they refused to specify what they'd encountered, however) and that they weren't staying in it. They also told the company that they could keep the deposit and keep the advanced three months rent money and all their belongings; they were out of there!

"They left a lot of really expensive furniture and a really nice pool table," says Claire. Her family put the items in storage and the couple was able to retrieve their belongings that way. "But when they left, they were leaving it all, they didn't even care," says Claire.

"Three [separate renters] left," says Claire, "none of us knew each other, and all of us said it was haunted."

In their search for a new home, Claire made sure that her husband was along for each showing, his intuitive radar intact, so they wouldn't end up in a home with any ghosts. They have gone through forty houses and finally found the right one; they will soon move into what they believe to be a ghost-free home.

The house on that rural Maysville Road has since been sold, but it still looks to be empty, says Claire. "There's no mailbox out front and you never see cars go in and out of the driveway. My dad's said he's never seen lights on."

Claire's not surprised. "It's haunted. That's why *we* don't live there anymore."

Chapter 25
The Sorg Opera House

The Sorg Opera House in Middletown, Ohio, brings to mind legendary movie stars like Gene Kelly and Marlena Dietrich. You can imagine patrons, dressed to the nines, entering the plush theatre, eagerly anticipating that night's operatic performance. It's as if history is oozing from its walls. Even now, when entering the theatre one can almost feel the past tango right up to greet them. The once-glamorous (and in the process of revisiting that grandeur again) structure was erected in 1891 and, as its name indicates, opera took center stage there for fourteen years. Following that, motion pictures were the main draw. The building found new purpose in 1985 as a theatre for staged productions. Now the site serves as the base for Road Apple Music, Miami Valley Idol competitions, movies, concerts in the ballroom, and according to theater Manager Dawn Rose of Road Apple Music's (and Switchcraft band member), it is in a constant state of evolution. The group is taking it one step at a time, however, working to revitalize the building and put the site to great use for the community. You get the vibe that there's something for everybody to enjoy at the Sorg. Yep, even for those who have already passed on. There are several ghosts at the Sorg; each with their own modus operandi.

Let's start from the top: If employee Heather Eacho never ventured up to the third balcony in the theater again, that would be too soon for her. She experienced real fear while up in that loft—the kind of fear that isn't fun, nor intriguing, but truly terrifying. Suffice to say, she's seen, heard, and felt things up there that she never wants to revisit.

The Sorg Opera House in Middletown, Ohio.

The third balcony in the theater is now blocked off, says Rose. It was where the African-Americans were segregated to watch the films, she adds with a shake of her head. They had their own entrance and exit, as well, which was separate from the others. Initials made in 1912 are carved into the wall by the once-segregated exit. This same exit always makes Rose "sick to her stomach" when she ventures down it, she says.

Rose shares that they are quite convinced that two of the balcony guests have returned despite their deaths. An African American man and an African American boy have been heard and seen. They do not seem to be happy spirits and Rose does not blame them, considering the injustices they experienced during their time on earth.

With some coaxing, Eacho bravely accompanied Rose and the author to the top balcony, but she didn't last long. She raced back down the stairs after seeing something shadowy moving in the projection room.

The balcony is not the only area in that massive theatre believed to have otherworldly inhabitants. It's also widely believed that Paul Sorg, the fellow the building is named after, hangs around backstage for the productions. He is usually seen directly on the stage area, where his office was, or up on the catwalks.

Eacho has seen a shadowy figure up on the catwalks backstage numerous times. So numerous, that she calls the specter "her boyfriend." This ghost, unlike the others, does not frighten her. In fact it is quite the opposite. Eacho is not certain if the ghost is, indeed, that of Sorg or if it's that of a stagehand; but she is certain he means no harm.

Eacho, however, does not feel the same camaraderie with the presence in the boiler room. Could be because it slammed the door shut on her, trapping her inside. Rose and Eacho mention that a medium said that what she saw in the boiler room was an elderly gentleman screaming, "Get out!" Even before they were told that, Rose and Eacho already got that vibe.

"They don't want you here," says Rose. "They are always saying for us to leave. The fiery redhead is evidently a no-nonsense woman. They aren't going to chase her away. She grins. "They don't want us around, but they aren't violent.""

An African-American man and boy haunt the third balcony at the Sorg.

There is also "a lady that appears in a blue ball gown," says Eacho, "but she doesn't bother me. You can see her better than the guy on the catwalk."

When Eacho began working at the Sorg, she wasn't in the dark; as far as the ghostly tales went. "I heard the stories about the place [being haunted]" admits Eacho, "but within the first or second show here, I had already seen something."

"We've had workers see them," Eacho adds. "One worker told me that 'he didn't believe it.' Then he looks up and sees my boyfriend above us on the catwalk," she adds with a grin. Now he believes it.

There are several spirits that Rose knows about. The two African Americans in the third floor balcony, the stagehand, Sorg, the presence in the boiler room, and the well-dressed, high-heel-wearing woman. "She has been seen in red, white, and blue dresses," says Rose.

Instead of evading the paranormal aspects of the building, the manager instead embraces it. So much so that Rose, Eacho, and a group of friends once decided to spend the night camping out on the stage. Rose lasted the entire night; very few others did. When they heard the female ghost walking in high heels up and down the stairs backstage "we lost about five people right then," says Rose with a hearty laugh. She has captured the sounds of the ghost's high heels walking back and forth on a video recording with sound. It's a fairly common occurrence to hear the lady roam the site.

Actually, the ghosts have been seen throughout the opera house. There are countless rooms and tunnels for them hang out in, after all. A ghost was banging on a bar downstairs relentlessly one night, says Rose. It was incredibly obnoxious and obvious. "They are just trying to get our attention," she says.

The Sorg auditorium.

Another night there was a show going on in the fourth floor ballroom, says Rose, and her friend went to take a picture of the band her boyfriend was playing in. Almost unbelievably, the band did not even appear in the photograph; all that was seen was a face floating above the stage. That isn't the only time the face has appeared either, says Rose. Other people have commented that they've seen a face that floats around up in that area. Even Eacho's nine-year-old son has had his own paranormal experience in the ballroom. He was playing one of the arcade games up there and asked his mother who the lady [in the gown] was, she says.

There are so many rooms in the historic structure and so many secrets left to uncover. Truth be told, Rose is having a blast taking it all in.

"We've been exploring a lot," she says. The structure is sound and they are all working on rejuvenating the building and bringing back its former grandeur.

"The ghosts don't like it at all when we start messing with things, but what are we gonna do? We have to restore it," Rose says with a shrug.

The ghost's obviously enjoy having a good time, as well. One of them even showed up for some nuptials. The owner's wife's son wedding took place there, and they had people come up to them and ask about "who the lady in the blue dress at the wedding was," says Rose. Of course there was no *human* in an old-fashioned long blue dress.

"It's very cool; I'm very open to it," says Rose. "I don't mind them being here. They were here first. I'm just trying to figure out why they're still here."

The Web site for Road Apple Music (in the Sorg): http://www.miamivalleyidol.com. The Sorg Opera House is located at 65 S. Main St. Middletown, Ohio 45044.

Chapter 26
Utopia

U topia, Ohio, is a ghost town that is still breathing so to speak; and in more ways than one. A handful of living residents remain in this town located in Clermont County, and if the legends are to be believed, over one hundred soaking-wet deceased residents are still roaming about its small-town streets as well.

Utopia is a place with a remarkable history. This tiny town abutting the Ohio River was used as a shipping port years ago, and in the early 1800s, there were no shortage of farmers utilizing the surrounding land. But its main claim to historic fame surrounds the two separate groups who lived there for a time.

A French fellow named Charles Fourier is credited for being the founder of Utopia. Fourier belonged to a religious group that was convinced that the globe was poised to enter a period of peace (35,000 years of it, to be exact) and that all of its inhabitants should be clustered into phalanxes (rather like a commune). These groups, traditionally, were self-contained and would measure around three miles in scope. The group would also provide the people with their own homes, land, stables, schools, and libraries—all for a fee of $25 per year.

Toss in the fact that this guy was certain that before long the ocean water would transform into lemonade and you've got a tart and unique beginning for this Utopia.

You might, however, have noticed that the oceans are still sans lemon. Well, so did Fourier's highly disappointed phalanx. The group as a whole reckoned that since the lemonade seas thing didn't happen, then what's to say that any of the other teachings were on the money? In 1846, the group disbanded, individual families left thirsting for the real truth. Whether they found it or not is anybody's guess.

Not long afterwards, John Wattles came to town. Wattles, a medium, was the leader of a group of spiritualists, and he was convinced Utopia would be the perfect place for his people to put down roots. After all, the group was searching for their utopia and they truly believed that this small Ohio town was the answer.

The spiritualists created an underground church so they could worship as they believed without fear of persecution. The incredible stone structure was buried twenty-five feet beneath the ground with a curved ceiling and two fireplaces. Although long ago abandoned and now locked/fenced off, the structure is still standing. The church measures eighteen feet wide, forty-four feet long, and twenty-two feet in height. Since it was constructed below the ground many people do not know it is there today, and sail right over/past it.

The rest of their buildings were above ground, however, and Wattles ordered that their three-level main dining hall, that Fourier's group had built, should be dismantled and erected right beside the Ohio River. Despite warnings about the potential for the river flooding from those who knew the area well, Wattles insisted that riverside dining was meant to be.

Longtime locals understood that the river depth and width could change drastically, and, at the time, Wattles group placed their hall on the river's edge site, it was at one of its lowest levels. Forging ahead, the phalanx project was undertaken one stone at a time and, ironically, concluded right before the great flood of 1847. Talk about bad timing (and bad mediums).

It was a wicked, rainy night, December 13, 1847, yet the spiritualists remained peppy and undaunted, celebrating their accomplishment in their building of wood and stone next to the grand Ohio. Then tragedy roared in, pulling their building and many of their lives right out from under them. Rain fell continuously, and suddenly there was a loud sound, loud enough that some of the spiritualists raced outside to see what it was. It was a huge wall of water barreling right towards them. Before they could react, the wood groaned, the walls gave way, and the building was ripped apart. Their dining hall, that they had spent many hours erecting,

quickly succumbed to a flash flood of epic proportions in seemingly an instant.

Unfortunately, although this group was devoted to Wattles, a
man they believed could contact spirits and get answers about the
future, he was unable to foresee the tragedy that would befall so
many of his people. Mother Nature plunged at least 100 spiritualists into the depths of the raging, frigid Ohio River. It is believed
only six persons made it out alive that fateful evening.

Some say these lost souls still today roam that riverbank where
the horrific flood occurred—being especially visible on stormy, dark
nights. The house where Reverend Wattles lived is also believed to
be haunted by up to six other otherworldly residents, the kicker
being that they are always soaking wet. The ghosts consist of a lady
in blue (a woman decked out in blue from hat to dress), a man in
a black hat and suit, three younger children, and a teenager.

Seems that all of these apparitions enter the Wattles' home
through the front door (like the rest of us). Once they're inside,
however, they disappear (unlike the rest of us). These sightings of
sopping wet spirits have been recorded ever since the great flash
flood happened. The same descriptions of the six individuals, the
same dripping wet scenarios, many times by people who had never
heard of others accounts beforehand.

Currently, it's been said that rainy nights in Utopia seem to
bring forth strange occurrences along the banks of the Ohio near
where the tragedy struck, as well as inside the former abode of
Wattles. People have reported seeing visions of the spiritualists
emerging from the water and/or drenched and roaming the banks
of the muddy river.

Andy Crosier and Shane Reinert filmed their Utopia segment
for *True Stories from Ohio with Richard Crawford*, at about nine o'clock
one Sunday night in August. While their guide/narrator went off
to retrieve the key to the padlock for the underground church, the
duo was stranded in the middle of nowhere, Utopia, Ohio, which
was a strange experience in its own right.

According to the filmmaking duo, the town at night felt undeniably eerie. "We're sitting out there wondering if he was ever
going to come back," says Reinert with a chuckle. "It was bizarre."
Of course their party eventually returned and they ventured into
the depths of the church to film.

"It's an underground church—twenty-five feet straight down and you have to use a wobbly ladder to get there," says Reinert. "It's like an underground gymnasium. It's peaked, the ceiling is curved, there's an earth floor, all stone walls and ceiling, and there are fireplaces in there. The church was hidden so they wouldn't be disturbed when performing their séances," adds the filmmaker.

The church was where the spiritualists would implore their medium, John Wattles, to help them contact their dead loved ones and/or the founding fathers of the country, even, to look for answers for their futures.

The church was manufactured so as to maintain a fairly constant temperature of around fifty-six degrees, year-round. This secret space for their church was vital as the spiritualists were extremely distrustful of society and those who were not part of their group. They knew that others outside of their clan would find great pleasure in disrupting and/or harassing them during their rituals. But what really happened within that cave-like structure day after day?

"When we were there, it looked like there were scratch marks on the ceiling of the church," says Reinert. "White lines—two or three together, looking like people were scratching to get out."

Over the years, townsfolk have reported seeing people, soaked to the bone, walking in the area toward the John Wattles House. "One woman was punched in the stomach while on a tour [by an unseen force]," standing outside the Wattles house, says Reinert, "and she was soaking wet after she got hit."

The Wattles house had no long-term residents (no more than seven years at a time) following this tragedy, until recently. Historian and narrator, Richard Crawford, stated on the DVD that he believes the Wattles house is one of the three most haunted sites in Clermont County, Ohio.

The film crew had their own strange events happen while in Utopia. While Reinert and Crosier were getting footage for the DVD, Crawford waited atop by the gate with the people who had the key to the structure. He was holding a square lantern.

"A weird thing happened then," says Reinert. Crawford pointed toward his lantern. "In the corner of the lantern was a drop of something red," says Reinert. "The candle was white. That red drop [was inside the glass] and appeared out of nowhere. It was like a drop of blood."

The underground church in Utopia. *Photo courtesy of Andy Crosier, Dark Figure Productions.*

How it got there and what it was is not known, but what is known is that the little town in Clermont County, Ohio, that is but a speck on the map, has an amazing history and just might contain more deceased "residents" than live ones.

Utopia may be small, but it is proud of its unique history.

Chapter 27
Blue Tower of Sorrow

There is a big bright blue stucco house with a tall tower in Waynesville, Ohio, that sits upon what used to be the main thoroughfare in town. From the outside, it looks like this is a manse that has definitely seen better days and is awaiting a renewal/rebirth of its initial magnificence. Whether this will happen is anybody's guess.

The home has undergone many manipulations since its inception in 1855. In addition to being a twenty-two-room single-family brick home (with a fireplace in each one of them), as well as having a built-in solarium, it has spent time as a nursing home and an apartment house. As is often the case with larger mansions from the past, they are revamped to fit the upcoming scenario, and this house is no exception. During the process of renovating the structure to be a nursing home, the original stairway was enclosed and a fire door was added.

The process of conversion has yielded the demise of much of the structure's grandness and glory, unfortunately. The back-arched breezeway that once led to the servants' quarters was blocked up. Wonderful stained-glass doorways were eliminated; cloaked with tacky new additions. The glorious tower that spanned toward the clouds was capped off with a tin roof. The massive, incredible garden that once covered an entire city block blooms no longer. The house appears forlorn, alone, rather like some of its past nursing home residents might have felt at times. It also appears to be haunted, and according to Waynesville historian, Dennis Dalton, it is.

A fellow named Hanes, a Quaker businessman from Cincinnati, built the house, which was a part of the Underground Railroad. There was a tunnel that came up the hill into the right side of the house into a room in the basement. The family watched for the slaves coming up the river valley from the top of that now dilapidated tower.

"The Hanes were very serious abolitionists and helped a lot of people escape through the Underground Railroad network here," says Dalton. "We don't know: Maybe the presences in this house are ghosts from that period of time."

"I knew the kids that lived here when it was last a residence, back in the early 1950s," says Dalton. "The iron gates are still all original. This house has had hauntings throughout its recent history. Water faucets go on and off all by themselves, lights go on and off."

Dalton explained that there seems to be a presence upstairs in one of the rooms. This presence can sometimes induce fear; other times not. "There have been some fairly serious things that have happened here," added Dalton, "just to let the people know hey, there's somebody else here." Given its eclectic history, it isn't shocking to learn that there are some unsettled spirits roaming about the house and grounds.

Dalton's uncle, Raymond Adams, who was superintendent of Miami Cemetery for many years, came to the residence and discovered that there was a grave in the yard. "Every year, in the spring, daffodils would come up around it," Dalton says. He did some research and it appears that a maid in this house during the Hanes' time, committed suicide on the site. "She drowned herself in a well in the back of the building over a jilted love affair."

It's been said that when the Hanes installed the furnace in this house, there was a dirt floor in the basement, and they had to dig down into the floor to get the furnace to fit in. Upon doing so, they found they'd uncovered multiple tombstones.

"Apparently, at some time or another, there was a small early cemetery on this property, and the Hanes didn't know it when they dug in to put in the foundation of the house," says Dalton. "If they would have known, they would have been sensitive enough, I'm sure, to have moved it."

The blue tower house was a stop on the Underground Railroad. Tombstones were uncovered in the basement of the structure.

The house with the twelve-foot ceilings and basement cemetery has been empty of living flesh for a long time. Nobody has raised a flag from the pole in the tower in years. Yet there is something living inside its historic walls. Something that has been around for a very long time and will likely always be.

Westwood Town Hall in Cincinnati, Ohio.

Chapter 28
Good Ol' Wesley

Westwood Town Hall in Cincinnati, Ohio, is very well taken care of. Not only by the current employees of the Cincinnati Recreation Commission, but also by its former caretaker, who just so happens to be a dearly departed ghost named Wesley. Turns out, Wesley became quite attached to the building while he was alive and took his duties very seriously. So much so, he simply has no inclination to leave the premises… even in death.

It is believed that when the town was annexed into Cincinnati, Wesley's position at the site was eliminated. Many guesstimate that it was this news, and/or the rejection of a woman that he loved that caused the man to toss a rope over a beam in the town hall's attic, put a noose around his neck, and drop away from his earthly life. Nobody knows how old Wesley was when he died, nor even his last name.

Wesley's glorious town hall, which has been a landmark in the Westwood neighborhood since its completion in 1889, is still a stunner today. It was built during the period of time when Westwood was an up and coming village, and they deemed it necessary to erect a site for their village offices, fire department services, and jail facilities.

The Cincinnati Recreation Commission is now in charge of the town hall and offers programs and forums for those of every age and interest. Local groups use the site for meetings and there is childcare offered there as well.

Area theater groups stage their plays at the charming century-old building and, while doing so, have been on the receiving end of some of Wesley's antics. He's been commonly known to hide props and play with lights. Yet that's not the half of it.

Wesley "introduced" himself to Marlene Trapp about six months after she took the position of Service Area Coordinator for the town hall, and he gave her a firsthand look at his wry sense of humor in the process. Trapp has been at Westwood since November of 2006, and was also there for several months in 2005.

"I knew a little bit about Wesley in the initial months," she notes, "but I can't say anything happened during that time." When Marlene was contacted by Dark Figure Productions to be part of their DVD project, however, she was told there were videotape copies of news stories done on Wesley. Trapp went looking for the videos but couldn't find them. She searched for weeks. One day, Trapp spent hours back in the storage area, sifting through hundreds of videos only to find none of the tapes she was looking for.

Frustrated, Trapp exited the storeroom and strolled into one of the main rooms that houses a television and VCR; both of them resting on a two-shelf cart. The equipment is utilized for a young, special needs child, who often watches children's videos there.

While passing through, Trapp did a double-take at the cart. She couldn't believe her eyes. Sitting right on the stand were two videos about Wesley.

"I said, 'Andrea [a coworker], they were on the *TV* stand all this time.'" But the coworker strongly disagreed. "She said, 'no they weren't. Nobody's watched these things for years.'"

Trapp says she jokingly replied, "'Okay, then I'm gonna believe Wesley put them there.'" She then left the room. Later, Trapp returned to the area with the television and was telling somebody about what happened only to look down and see yet another video about Wesley sitting on top of the others.

"Okay, I KNOW that one wasn't there when I picked the other two up," she had said aloud. "I really believe now."

The other staff members already believed, thank you very much. They've encountered his shenanigans repeatedly throughout the years. Turns out, Wesley is particularly fond of playing with water.

"You're in the bathroom and you're the only one in there and the water faucet turns on by itself," claims the Westwood Town Hall crew.

"When I come out of the stall the water will be running," says seven-year employee Victoria Scott, "and that's the first thing I do when I walk in there is look at the sink [to be sure it isn't on]." Wesley also enjoys messing with the office machinery.

"Before I even put anything in the copier, here comes a piece of paper out and it's got words on it but there's nothing up at the top," says Scott.

"It's true," chimes in Andrea McCarthy, who has been an employee at Westwood for ten years. "He copied a whole page she didn't even have on there."

The children at the site are not afraid of Wesley. In fact, it is quite the contrary. They enjoy the thought that he is around, watching over them. The younger kids do see things (full-body apparitions) and do ask questions. "We just say that we 'pretend' it's a ghost," the staff says.

"I have the preschoolers," says McCarthy, "and this time it was little boys and they said, 'Miss Andrea, what's that man doing?' They said they saw a man, and he walked down the hall." Wesley, perhaps? "It's not as creepy as it used to feel, but there are still times when you walk into the building and get that creepy feeling," she adds.

Seems Wesley isn't the only ghost hanging around the hall, either. "You can hear a male and a female voice talking [down the hall]," says McCarthy. "We had a group of psychics do a walk-through in the building and they said that there is a lady named Mary in the building, too. They also said that they believe that Wesley was extremely distraught."

Wesley makes himself known when he feels like it. "It's usually when you aren't expecting it to happen," says Scott.

Anybody that is at the site for longer than a few days is likely to encounter something strange, according to the crew. The employees that have been there for more than a brief time have all experienced unexplainable events. The door that was locked is open, the lights that were off are on, and those pesky water faucets start flowing out of the blue.

McCarthy knew about Wesley before she signed on to work at Westwood Hall. "When I first started working here, I came in here and said, 'Wesley I strongly believe this is your territory and you can play any jokes you want on me, but I don't want to physically see you.'" So far so good. "The first night I had to lock up the building by myself, I called my husband and said 'get up here!'" McCarthy grins and adds, "If I actually see something, I think I would freak."

The younger children have claimed to see a man, other people have seen shadows, etc., and several local television stations have done stories about Wesley. People have witnessed shadows looking out of the attic windows. It is believed that Wesley might have been staring out the windows the night he died—heartbroken, watching the love of his life leave him forever.

Doors have opened spontaneously. The area where the kiln used to be kept is said to have a very strange vibe to it. It has been claimed by a psychic that it is actually a portal to another dimension. People who have worked there claim that they felt a strange sensation at the kiln, like they could be pulled inside.

Former employee, Tammi Nuber, said in an email that her favorite story occurred years ago with a little boy named Robby.

"We were in the day camp room off the kitchen in the basement playing with [little toy] cars on the floor when Robby rolled a car under the door that leads to the back hallway where that bathroom was," writes Nuber.

"Well, Wesley had always been protective over that door, and no matter if you had the right key or not, it would only open for certain people. So we called over another counselor and he whispered to the door, 'Come on, Wesley, let us in, Robby lost his car.' Well, of course the door unlocked and we went in to get the car. The car was nowhere to be found and there was nothing but a toilet and sink in this area. The car, which I saw with my own eyes go under the door was missing. We told Robby we would get him another car and left the hallway, shutting the door behind us. Not more than ten seconds later the car came rolling out from under that door. Freaky, huh?" Nuber shares that Wesley seemed to be particularly attached to little Robby. "He followed him everywhere."

Another event remains ensconced in Nuber's mind. "Once Robby went into the boys bathroom downstairs, and the next thing [I heard], Robby is screaming for me. I went to see what was wrong and when I got there, all the sinks were running cold water and the entire bathroom was steamed up." Cold water and steamed up windows? How is that possible? It appears that only Wesley knows.

This is now merely a maintenance area, but once served as the jail. Strange things have been reported in the basement, and some believe there is a portal there (check out the weird image to the right of the door).

"There were many, many times that I would turn all the lights off, lock the building and when I would get into my car, I would look up and the lights would go on in the attic or preschool and ballet rooms upstairs," Nuber writes. "Wesley liked to play games with me quite often. He would call from one phone to another when I knew I was the only one in the building, and he constantly locked me out of rooms."

"We also tried to conjure [Wesley] up with a Ouija Board," shares Nuber. He did not like that at all. We would find the board outside on cars, picnic tables, in the grass, never in the closet where we left it."

If things go missing or Trapp needs to locate something she says she calls on the caretaker for aid: "Wesley, please help me find it." Most of the time that is exactly what this long-departed but devoutly present Westwood Town Hall employee does. Good Ol' Wesley…

Westwood Town Hall is located at 3017 Harrison Avenue in Cincinnati, Ohio.

Marlene Trapp, Service Area Coordinator for the Cincinnati Recreation Commission says that Wesley is a welcome "employee" that has been known to help her out in a pinch.

Chapter 29
Big Bone Lick Park

Heaven only knows where a specter or disembodied voice can pop up. A dank basement of a 200-year-old house? Sure. The back room of a tavern that was once a hub of illicit and illegal activities? Sounds darn likely. How about throughout a gorgeous, 546-acre park, much of it registered with the National Register of Historic Places? (What?) You betcha! Such is the case for Big Bone Lick State Park in Union, Kentucky, a habitat that has been rumored to be haunted for many years.

When you first visit the park, you wouldn't likely expect that there has been so much paranormal activity taking place. Nonetheless, year after year, there have been numerous accounts of unexplained sights and sounds all throughout the acreage, everything from full-bodied apparitions to little girls' voices to light shows of the paranormal kind.

The park's name is translated from the Shawnee Native American tribe, which named the park Big Bone Lick because of its salt spring deposits. It is a nationally recognized treasure and an official stop on the Lewis and Clark trail. This area holds not only the bones but also, perhaps, the spirits of a long-ago time.

A time during the Pleistocene Epoch era when wooly mammoths, musk ox, and giant sloths (and those who hunted them) were drawn down south toward the warm salt springs bubbling forth from within the earth; when a massive sheet of ice covered the earth from the Ohio River all the way north to Canada.

The salty springs were a magnet for massive animals, some of which ended up dying entrapped within what was once called "jelly ground." Their skeletal remains were left behind and were first uncovered in 1739. Since that time remains from the site have since been exhibited at museums across the globe. Both Benjamin Franklin and Thomas Jefferson knew the area quite well and had personally examined the fossils from the park. These incredible fossils have been shipped across America and studied by many. There are more bones, as well, that just might be revealed one day.

Big Bone is the site where, in 1795, Mary Inglis was able to escape the clutches of the Shawnee and embark upon her amazing trip home to Virginia.

Although highly depleted now, the Big Bone salty springs are still present in this park, recognized by the scientific world as the "Birthplace of American Vertebrate Paleontology."

Certainly, the park is worth a visit on its own right; it holds a plethora of activities and sights to see, including a lake for fishing, campground, dense wooded areas (if you dare), a herd of bison, a community and nature center, the Big Bone Lick Museum, and a self-guided trail that educates walkers as they stroll through portions of the park. True to form for the paranormal subject, it also has a cemetery.

It's a one of a kind place, all right, and perhaps that is why so many refuse to leave; even after they've departed their earthly plains.

According to an article in the *Boone County Recorder* by Paul McKibben, dated October 26, 2006, some locals and even some of the park employees believe that something unexplainable has been going on for years at this incredible locale. So much so that the park's naturalist, Todd Young, led a group of over fifty individuals on what looks to be a one-time, unique tour on a crisp, October night.

One of the buildings on site is the Big Bone Methodist Church, circa the nineteenth century. This white wooden structure illuminates the entrance area of the park's grounds with its impressive stature. The church has been well taken care of and the strength of the faithful that erected the building still reverberates across the parkland. Additionally, it appears that footsteps also reverberate from the upper floor, even when no one (human, that is) is found to be upstairs. The organ on the second floor has also been known to suddenly play by itself, this is noted at something that would strike a chord of fear in most people.

Another building on site is the Park Nature Center. Volunteers at the center have claimed that they've heard a small girl's voice calling out inside the structure. In the newspaper account, Young admitted to hearing voices in the nature center along with the volunteers and employees, and said he does not know whom they belonged to. It's a mystery.

The park naturalist in the *Recorder* article, also indicated that he has witnessed shadows and "balls of light go across" the field. He does not know what they are. Locals have told Young that they've witnessed human shapes pacing in the field after dark.

Native Americans who were camping at the park for the annual Salt Festival, reported rising one morning and witnessing other Native Americans traversing through the field by the park's entrance, dressed in the Native American garb that was worn long ago. No other Native Americans were present at the time, so the sightings were unexplainable.

Big Bone Lick State Park is filled with fossils, history, and if the many accounts are to believed, a vast conglomeration of hauntings, as well.

Big Bone Lick State Park is located at 3380 Beaver Road in Union Kentucky. Web site: http://parks.ky.gov/stateparks/bb/.

The old Methodist Church at Big Bone Lick has been the site of unexplained footsteps, and the organ has been heard playing by itself on the second floor.

There was a triple murder on this land back in 1879, and it's been nigh on impossible keeping tenants there for any length of time since.

Chapter 30
For Rent

The axe fell on South Main Street in Waynesville, Ohio before midnight in late August, 1879. It fell far too many times for anyone to survive and the gruesome result was the murder of three innocents—two women and an eleven-year-old girl. They lay, massacred, undiscovered in their own congealed blood, for a week. Given this fact, it is not surprising to learn that the infamous triple axe murder has reverberations that continue to ring forth now. Even though that house has been torn down and a new one stands in its place, the vibes of the violence that took place on the land have not been altered. Spirits remain and they are heard from.

In the summer of 2007, the green one-story with the stenciled shutters on South Main Street stands empty; the metal prongs of the neon red "For Rent" sign sunk deep into the front lawn. It's a sign that appears to go unheeded. It's been months. This home is a nondescript place; nothing would single it out as anything special, nor anything sinister. The house that stood there before it, however, is a far different story. The interior of that home was all but smothered with the aftermath of murder.

In 1897, a two-story home stood tall upon that spot closely abutting the road. The house was being rented out back then to a family whose names and horrific manner of death would go down in Ohio history.

The trio would die by the hands of someone they knew; by a relative. It was the piercing stench that alerted neighbors and authorities that something was not right inside that home. The smell of death crept under the doorways and permeated through the windows and walls. It was, after all, not just one death but three.

Imagine the victims' shock and horror as each one was bludgeoned to death, one after the other, by a family member—eighteen-year-old Willie Evert Anderson, wearing a handmade mask over his face, fastened with string.

One of the women was found in a pool of blood in the hallway, the other was attacked in bed, and the other victim was "chopped up" and discovered further down the same hallway. So much horror and pain that even when the old house was torn down and a new house built, the figurative stench of death still permeated the site.

Why did Willie and, likely, an accomplice, create a bloodbath of epic proportions in this wonderfully quaint small town? Why did Willie murder his mother, thirty-seven-year-old Mollie Hatte, his aunt St. Clem Weeks, and Myrtle Edith Shaw, his eleven-year-old cousin?

According to newspaper accounts of that time, throughout his young life, Willie found the subjects of violence and murder endlessly fascinating, and he felt strongly compelled to traverse the dark and insidious path of a killer firsthand. Throughout his life, it was written in the local paper, this young man was acknowledged as a fellow who could keep a secret and would do so no matter how small or large that secret might be. Usually that is a well sought after character trait but not when it came to confession as to who his murderous accomplice was. He refused to spill the beans.

It was also noted that a pungent lack of remorse was evident in Anderson. What was even stranger was that his father was very well known and respected in Waynesville—a man who penned his thoughts and memories which ultimately aided in documenting the history of the town.

Waynesville town historian, Dennis Dalton, remarks that "they never could get the bloodstains out of the floor [of the original house]. They would think that they had them all cleaned up only to return and find the bloody stains coming through once again," Dalton shares. It was like a testament from the murdered women and young girl that what happened here could and should never be forgotten.

Dalton says that his mother, who was born in 1911, told him that nobody could live in the house after the murders, not only because of the bloodstains, but also because of the strange and highly unsettling sounds that people would hear.

"There were loud noises from upstairs like somebody pushing heavy things or dropping something on the floor," Dalton says. "I often say 'it's the axe falling,'" he adds.

A while back, the current house was built smack dab on the same site. In fact, part of the house covers the bedroom where the one woman was murdered. Several years ago, a couple was living in the home with their three daughters, says Dalton.

"The older daughter and mother were in the kitchen one summer evening washing the supper dishes. They had their backs to the doorway. The original dining room was there," Dalton says, pointing to the center of the home.

"All of the sudden, as the mother/daughter talked, they got this peculiar feeling and the hair on nape of their necks just rose up and the hair on the back of their arms straightened out," he continues. "They put down their dishtowels, turned around and not ten feet from them, standing just in front of the door, was the figure of a Victorian woman. She was holding the hand of a small girl dressed in the same style."

The mom and child [the living pair] were so startled they couldn't move; they could hardly breathe, for that matter, and "suddenly, those ghostly figures who looked neither right nor left just sort of glided or floated across the floor past the mother and daughter within just a few feet of them and dissolved through the north wall of the building—all while they watched," Dalton says.

Was that St. Clem and her daughter, Myrtle? No one knows for sure. All that is known for sure is that the triple Anderson murders on South Main Street have left their mark in the town's history books and upon the land upon which the gruesome acts occurred.

Dalton points to the "For Rent" signs and adds, "It's empty. Well, it's *technically* empty right now."

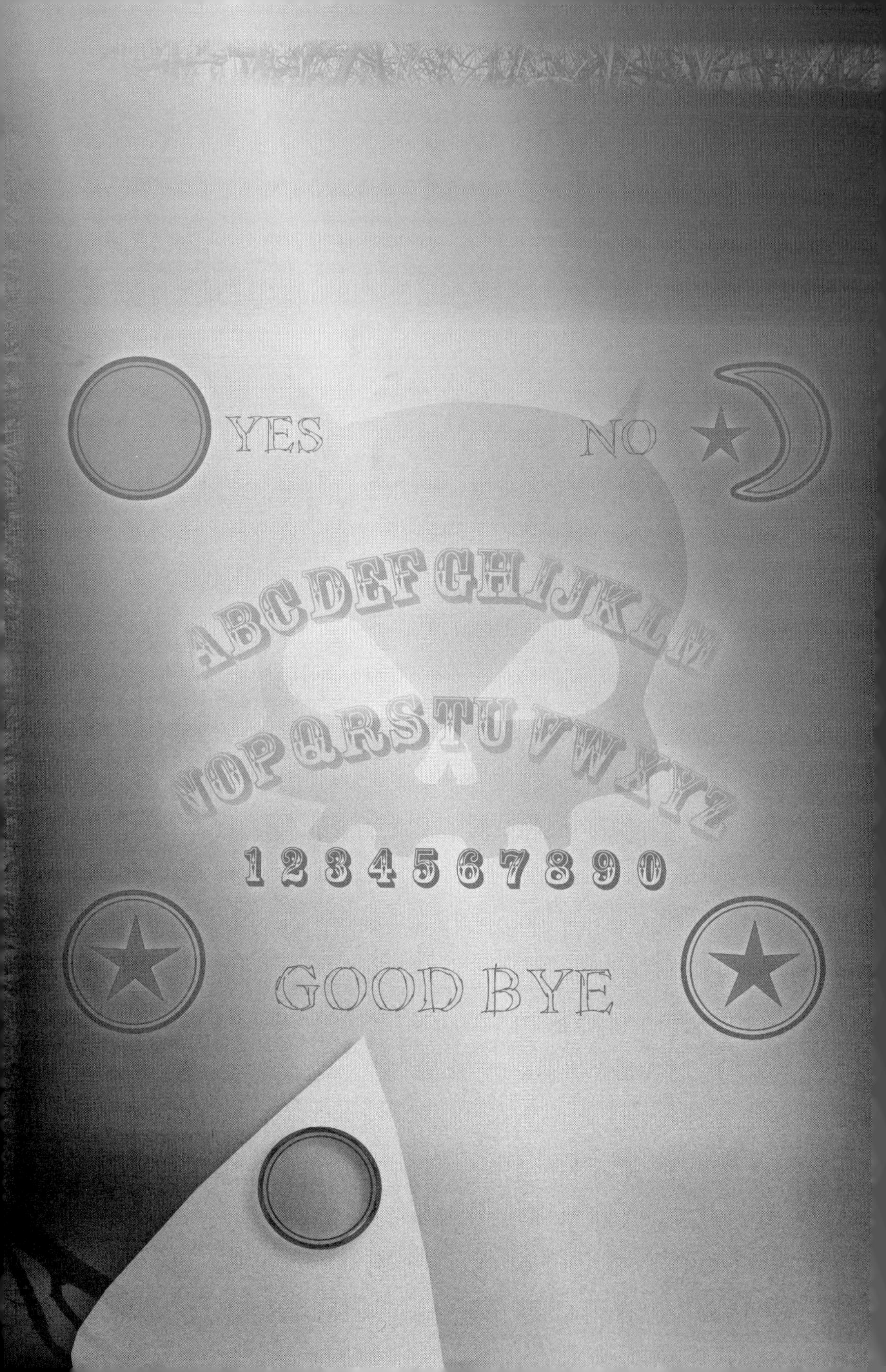
YES
NO
ABCDEFGHIJKLM
NOPQRSTUVWXYZ
1234567890
GOOD BYE

Chapter 31
Don't Mess with Ouija

Ann Brandon/Angel/Ouija Board

Ann Brandon has always been particularly sensitive to the world around her. She gets vibes, feelings or thoughts, whatever you might want to call them about certain things, and often they are right on the money. Brandon has accepted that this is part of her norm. It might happen while Brandon is undergoing a ghost hunting investigation with the group Paranormal Investigators of Northern Kentucky (PINK). She might "feel" what the presence feels and/or whether the presence is a man, woman, or child. But it doesn't stop there: Brandon is just as likely to feel the need to relay something to a friend or family member, or to call someone she's been thinking about—at the precise time they are needing her.

Sometimes Brandon's feelings and debunking efforts, in conjunction with her teammates at PINK, help others come to a resolution about what inhabits their home or business and helps to give them closure. Sometimes, this intuitive gift can help Brandon, herself, achieve the same blessed thing.

An example of this happened in 2002. It turned out to be one of the most excruciating years of this northern Kentucky resident's life. That was the year her mother and father each passed away within one month of each other, of unrelated issues.

"It kind of made me stop and think, life is too short, it was really a great growth period," she shares. Brandon credits her trauma for helping direct her life to her current position helping her gender start anew at a local women's crisis center.

That's not to say that this period of time wasn't incredibly hard for this warm-hearted woman with a wry sense of humor, because it undoubtedly was. There was a sense of contemplation elicited from her parent's passing, however, and it ultimately changed the course of her life.

The mother-daughter bond is one that can be felt even when one of the pair has died. Brandon discovered this firsthand, courtesy of an angel. A trinket angel, that is.

Brandon inherited her mother's curio cabinet after her passing and one day she happened to notice that a particular angel seemed to be shifting its position around the cabinet.

"This angel keeps moving!" Brandon thought. "It *is* moving, right? Am I crazy?" One day the angel would be facing one way, the next day it would be in the opposite direction. She laughs and says, "I would move it back." The curio cabinet has a lock on it, says Brandon, and it is not a piece of furniture that is easily opened, so she was completely perplexed as to how this was happening.

When her best friend, Brooke, came to visit Brandon one day, she couldn't resist telling her, "I know my mom is moving the angel in the curio cabinet. I just know she is!"

Her friend, who is also a spiritual person, said, "Okay, let's do an experiment." Brandon explains that she's known her friend since she was eleven years old and that she is very honest and of a similar nature as her own. Bottom line: She has Brandon's complete trust. Together the two said a prayer and they said, "Mom, if it's really you; move the angel."

The pair then had something to eat and chatted about this and that for the next hour-and-a-half—up until Brooke glanced over at the curio. A huge intake of breath followed.

"Oh my God!" Brooke squealed. The angel was completely turned the other way, says Brandon. "We jumped up and down and cried. There was true emotion there and it was just a wonderful thing." The intenseness of the incident was indelibly profound to both of the women.

"It hasn't moved since then, though," says Brandon, adding that she just can't help herself from checking to see if it moved when she enters the room to this day.

Prior to her angelic experience, Brandon went through an amazing journey, courtesy of the Ouija Board. It was nighttime in the late 1980s: Brandon was in college in Indiana, hanging out with her friends, and it was one of the several occasions when they decided to use the Ouija Board.

"It still gives me the willies to talk about it," Brandon shares. "I don't want to do any more experiments with it now, but at this point, I did."

It should be noted that this, again, was a particularly tough time in Brandon's life; her parents were getting a divorce, she was wondering about her biological genus, and she was a fragile freshman in college to boot. Her emotional state was tender and raw.

On this particular evening, Brandon recalls that her roommate asked the board for information about Brandon's biological mother. It didn't take long before a last name was spelled out (one that was NOT a common name in any sense of the word), followed letter-by-letter with the first name, the much more common, Karen.

"By now, I'm starting to freak," says Brandon. The roommate then asked the board to spell out where this Karen woman lives. The letters *O X F O R D* appeared.

"I was thinking, Oxford? Oxford, London? What is this? You know?" says Brandon. Her friend asked for clarification and then the board spelled out *OH*. Ohio.

Turns out that Oxford, Ohio, was not very far from their Indiana college town. Inspired by the emotion in the room, the roommate continued querying the Ouija Board, next asking if there was a phone number. The board replied: "*NO PHONE*."

Brandon admits that at this point in the juncture, she was wondering what she might be getting herself into here and thinking "Okay, this isn't funny."

Despite the fact that it was rapidly nearing midnight, her roommate called information to see if there are any other people with that same last name in Oxford, Ohio. They were hooked up to a person with that same last name directly in Oxford, Ohio. It was a man who picked up the phone, however. Brandon's roommate told him it was an emergency. She asked him if he knew of, or was related to a woman named Karen, with the same last name as his.

The man (who thankfully was not agitated upon being phoned at that late hour) replied, "Well, yeah, that's my sister."

When further questioned as to whether his sister had a phone number, the man replied that she had no phone. He added that she lived right down the street, however.

"I was literally going through all of these emotions," admits Brandon. "I'm crying and freaking out saying things like 'a Ouija Board just found my birth mom!'" It was an emotional roller coaster of the paranormal kind.

"Do you want to talk to her?" the man had said. "I'll go down and get her." They told him that yes, they needed to talk with her.

"So the brother goes down and gets her and she gets on the phone, and I can't speak—I have to have my roommate talk to her (I was just too flabbergasted)," says Brandon. "I'm thinking, oh my God, I just found my birth mother!"

Still undaunted, Brandon's roommate proceeds to ask the clueless woman named Karen, "Did you have a baby December 3, 1967?"

Almost unbelievably, the woman replied, "Yes."

"I started bawling and crying when I heard that," says Brandon.

Perplexed, Karen responded, "Why [do you want to know]?"

Brandon's roommate replied, "Well, my friend here thinks that you might be her birth mother."

After a short pause Karen said to the college friends, "Wait a minute! Are y'all white?"

"Yes…" came their reply.

"Well, I ain't had no white baby!" Karen retorted.

Oops. Wrong birth mom.

The Ouija Board must have a mean sense of humor to send this collegiate troupe on such a wild goose chase that included precise and correct information about this woman's name, lack of phone, residence in Oxford, Ohio and, most amazingly, the birth date of her child. The only problem was, the woman was African American and Brandon is Caucasian.

"That is pure evil," Brandon says with a laugh. "Evil! Okay, it's funny now that I think about it, but at the time it was horrifying and I never touched a Ouija Board again." Brandon has since located her real birth mother, and did not turn to a Ouija Board to do it.

Chapter 32
A Peek Inside the 20ᵗʰ Century Theatre

T he 20ᵗʰ Century Theatre in Cincinnati initiated an innovative series of firsts when it came to design and treatment of patrons, and now it just might be the first (and only?) theatre to have its own deceased projectionist, Herman, on permanent patrol within its art deco expanse. Given the theatre's grandeur, no wonder this fellow would not want to leave this luxurious haven.

The doors to the Twentieth Century first swung open for business in 1941. The theatre was designed in the Neoclassical Modern style in a way to not only wow its patrons with its gleaming architecture, but just as importantly, to impart wonderful acoustics, which was not of major concern to other theatre designs at that time. It was the first theatre to offer free valet parking and it was also the first theatre to be air-conditioned in Cincinnati.

The brightest and most prominent stars of their day graced the big screen at the Twentieth, but alas, this brilliant gem faded in customers' eyes with the birth and subsequent explosion of the multiplex theatre. Most neighborhood movie houses were left in the dust, and the 20ᵗʰ Century Theatre, too, fell victim to the growing trend. It closed its doors in 1983.

For years, this incredible landmark was left unattended, allowed to crumble beneath the uncompromising wrath of Mother Nature and vandals, enduring water leaks, neglect, and apathy. For half of a decade, members of the community debated which scenario was best: To bulldoze the structure or restore the theatre to its former glory.

Seven years or so after its abandonment, a local businessman bought the building, planning to restore it and use it as a retail establishment. A floor company occupied the building for a year and then moved to a different site. Following that, an area church took over occupancy of the building for around four years.

The 20th Century Theatre in Cincinnati, Ohio.

20th Century Theatre was brought into the twenty-first century by its current occupant; 20th Century Productions, which is owned by Mark Rogers (who also owns the haunted Habits restaurant and bar across the street). The theatre plays host to Special Concert Events and private functions, and has done so since October 23, 1997.

It also came complete with an extra added bonus: A resident projectionist who happens to be dead.

Herman was the projectionist at 20th Century for years when he was suddenly stricken with a heart attack while working. The poor fellow passed away right up there in the projectionist's booth.

Strange, unaccountable things have occurred since Herman's demise and those who are privy to the history of the theatre have taken to attributing these events to the dedicated projectionist.

One of the VIP rooms at the glamorous 20th Century Theatre.

One of the first "people" to notice something strange was happening in that booth was an adorable fellow named Strider—the resident dog. When first entering the building, the theatre's fluffy little unofficial mascot would refuse to ascend the theatre's balcony stairs into the projectionist area. Instead, his white and black paunches remained solidly planted on the floor below, dark eyes staring up at the open door, repeatedly barking at the unseen male within its confines. Since that time, Strider has gradually adjusted to this area of the theatre (and to Herman, perhaps?) and will now enter the projectionist area without so much as a nip or yip.

Brian Robbins, Events Manager for the 20ᵗʰ Century Theatre, is reluctant to verify or expound upon his personal encounters because he believes they are too vague to be sensational. However, Robbins clearly recalls a strange incident that happened when the house was hopping during a comedy event. The comedian on stage had playfully ordered a shot of tequila to toast the crowd. Robbins obtained two shots from the bar in the lobby (so he could participate in the toast) and was reentering the main performance room when he saw "and felt" a dark figure right in his path. "I almost bumped into something," he recalls. He uttered "excuse me," and only then realized that there was now nobody next to him. What or whom had he felt/seen? He has no clue, but he does know that it could not have been human, because in a flash, the figure disappeared. Thankfully, Robbins was able to quickly compose himself and the toast ensued as planned.

Theatre owner Rogers says that he periodically hears of strange accounts from employees and/or patrons, but he hasn't experienced a whole lot of unexplained events himself. Rogers does recall, however, experiencing something weird while showing the theatre to a couple who was considering renting the establishment for their upcoming wedding.

Since the theatre's bread and butter hails mostly from weddings and private events, this was an important appointment to Rogers, and he was upset with himself for forgetting to turn on the music in the theatre before the couple had arrived. Rogers usually makes it a point to pipe music in the background to help set the lush romantic ambience and showcase the theatre's fine acoustics.

Chiding himself internally at first, but ultimately forgetting about it, Rogers began walking the couple around, pointing out the many attributes of the grand place. Then out of nowhere, lilting tunes suddenly and magically filled the air.

"The music came on by itself," says Rogers with a grin. The couple noticed the lyrical aural addition and they all shared a laugh. Granted, Strider's one smart pooch, but it's doubtful that he was that smart. It's rather nice to believe that it was Herman, helping his "boss" out in a pinch.

The 20th Century Theatre is located at 3021 Madison Road, Cincinnati, Ohio 45209. Web site address: www.the20thcenturytheatre.com.

The adorable "Strider" was one of the first "people" to notice that something was hanging out in the projection area of the theater, according to events manager, Brian Robbins.

Chapter 33
Angel of the Garden

W hen you're in the mood for quaint charm, delectable sandwiches, desserts, heavenly tea—oh, and, perhaps some heavenly visitors—the Angel of the Garden Tea Room & Gifts in Waynesville, Ohio, is the place for you. Built in 1901 and open for business as a teahouse since February of 1997, it is a true treasure, tucked into a town brimming with history and remarkable stories.

Owner Pam McNeily, her sister, Vickie Roberts, and a few other members of the clan know how to concoct a tea room right. Dennis Dalton, the one non-family member (but only in the blood-relation sense of the word) is the special events coordinator and storyteller extraordinaire. Toss in not one, nor two, but three otherworldly tea-room visitors, and you've got one heck of an interesting reception committee.

McNeily recalls first noticing unexplainable activity when she started doing renovation on the charming site. Whether it was the noise involved with the process or the change, it definitely stirred the paranormal pot. Strange sounds, smells, and the unexplained followed.

McNeily said that the occurrences seem to happen in bunches, as well. They might have several of them daily for several weeks and then have nothing out of the ordinary happen for months.

"The most noticeable thing about it," said McNeily, "is that it seems like it's always on a Tuesday." Her sister, Vickie grins and nods in agreement. As for the explanations behind the hauntings, it is Dalton who has spent much time uncovering the past of the teahouse. It comes naturally to him because in addition to his duties at the teahouse, Dalton is Waynesville's resident historian; harboring delectable town tidbits as enticing as the Angel of the Garden's crumpets themselves. This jovial and intelligent fellow has over a century of historic facts and scenarios clearly designated inside his often grinning head, and can spout this information freely, without any need for notes or books. He has been giving local historical tours since 1978, and providing walking ghost tours (The Not so Dearly Departed Tour) since the 1980s.

The former library employee also knows the past goings on in Waynesville, Lebanon, Springboro, and much of Warren County, as well. No wonder he fits in so well at the tea room.

"I have a distinct feeling I belong here," says Dalton. McNeily and Roberts agree.

The house the tea room inhabits dates back to 1901, but Dalton did his research (of course!) and discovered that there was another home on the site, occupied by a hard-cussing, no-nonsense-taking woman named Betsy Ridge. Dalton is quite confident that Betsy is one of the three ghostly inhabitants.

To make things even more interesting about the house, a man's skeleton had been found in the attic in the 1960s; along with a box full of what appeared to be human hair.

McNeily shudders, wondering whom the body was—nobody will ever know, she says. She also ponders the reason anybody would stockpile a pile of human hair. The house definitely has its share of weird eccentricities that both lived and died there.

They also believe another woman that lived on the site, Mary Cornell, has stayed put, too. In addition there is a dapper fellow that hangs around (so to speak) that McNeily's son witnessed walking straight out of a wall. They are not sure who this fellow is since several men lived—and died there—including Charles Cornell, Mary Cornell's husband. Also in residence for years was Dr. Witham, whose office occupied what is now the dining room of the establishment. A fellow named Sam Meredith, a tobacco buyer, was another of the fellows who once lived at the home.

Dalton has also noted that the female ghosts at the tea room "make stronger impressions," which is why he believes that they don't know precisely who the male ghost is.

The scent of orange blossoms often precipitates a visit from beyond, which McNeily finds particularly wonderful. She grew up in California and being enveloped by the sublime citrus blossom aroma is a treasured memory from her and her sister's child-hood. How strange that such an aroma would permeate a home in Waynesville, Ohio, however.

Speaking of which, the home and all its surrounding land are potential targets for an unexpected visit, including out on the decks and in the backyard rose garden.

There have been full-blown apparitions, like the one McNeily's son witnessed, as well as glimpses of "people" through the front and side windows walking up to the door only to find nobody there.

They have also noticed strange lights floating high up in the corners and the sounds of a very lively party trailing down from the third floor. Someone outside saw an image of a mournful man staring out at them from the back upper floor window. The family has heard nonexistent dishes being forcibly set down on the counter in the kitchen while they were all together, talking in the parlor.

One of her more recent encounters happened when McNeily awoke to find the transparent outline of a person floating beneath the blades of the upper bedroom ceiling fan.

It's not only the people that work in or visit the tea room who have seen things, either. Their neighbor has reported hearing a woman's voice early in the morning coming from the house, which has not been McNeily or her sister. They do not live onsite. And a carpenter, working inside the home by the fireplace suddenly "felt" like somebody was right next to him, and after it began moving in closer, and closer still, he bolted out the door. They found him, shaken, awaiting their return outside on the front veranda.

One of the most memorable occurrences for Dalton took place in the tea room kitchen. A large, lidded pot was setting on the stove and he was chatting on the phone about Mary Cornell with a descendant of the Cornell family.

"It's just too bad this poor soul had this grumpy personal-ity," he recalls having said. No sooner had Dalton uttered those prophetic words than the lid that had been perched atop the pot suddenly flew high up in the air, flipped over, and slammed back down onto the vessel.

Point taken, said Dalton. Although this gregarious man is not one to become frightened at ghosts or unknown things, he admits that that one, particular episode probably came the closest to test-ing his nerves. It also made him realize how important it is to show respect to the spirits in our midst.

Angel of the Garden Tea Room & Gifts in Waynesville, Ohio.

"It was profound," he shares. Now Dalton will periodically say things like, "Mrs. Cornell, is this all right?" when undertaking something he thinks she might have an opinion about, which most likely pleases Mary to no end.

"It's their house, after all," says Dalton. McNeily nods in agreement.

"We don't know about the afterlife," admits the amiable historian, "but we speculate that these beings would react the way we would. If we experience anger or distaste [why wouldn't they, as well]?" He grins and adds, "I spend more time talking with the dead than with the living. And believe me, it's not the dead we have to fear; it's the living."

McNeily and the others like to think that the ghosts not only accept them being there, but appreciate them being there. "We often hear sounds of a party or a dance, times when they were the happiest," notes McNeily.

Christmastime, for example is "very active," she shares, and that is when the Angel of the Garden Tea Room is bustling with festivity and joy.

"We have lots of social activities and special events (how about tea with the characters from *Alice in Wonderland*?)," says McNeily. "I think they approve what we do here."

"We have a very positive feeling in this place," said Dalton. "We feel our ghosts are looking over us and taking care of their property. We're just their twenty-first century characters. It's theirs, and we work around it. It's part of our legacy. We love it."

For further information about the Angel of the Garden Tea Room or to book a "Not so Dearly Departed Tour" with Dennis Dalton you can log onto: Angelofthegarden.com. Located at 71 N. Main Street Waynesville, Ohio 45068 – 1144.

Bobby Mackey's Nightclub in Wilder, Kentucky.

Chapter 34
Bobby Mackey's

"Warning to our Patrons: This establishment is purported to be haunted. Management is not responsible and cannot be held liable for any actions of any ghost/spirits on the premises."

You get an idea that Bobby Mackey's Music World is not your typical honky-tonk from the moment you step inside the door. The first clue is the bright yellow sign, bearing the aforementioned warning on the front wall. Not one of your usual nightclub notices, to be sure.

"Oh, they're here," says Donna Clifton, longtime manager of the club located in Wilder, Kentucky. "There's no doubt in my mind. I believe it. I've had too many things happen to me not to believe it."

Considering the fact that Mackey's is renowned across the globe for being one of the most frighteningly haunted sites, let alone taverns, it's not too much of a shocker to hear that they are just as apt to have people come hoping to see something paranormal as they are for people to come hear the talented Bobby Mackey sing and strum. Sometimes people who come strictly for the music get more than they bargained for.

"We got sued," says Clifton. "Sued for $500 for the clothes that got ripped up on some guy [by a ghost in a cowboy hat] while he was in the bathroom." The suit was eventually thrown out, but Mackey's attorney insisted that the sign go up.

The tavern is next to the railroad tracks and a hop, skip, and a jump from the Licking River. The Licking River and the Nile are two of only a handful of rivers that flow north in the world, says Mackey's go-to employee, Matt Coates. Strange and fitting somehow.

So…what's it like working at a tavern with such an incredibly haunted reputation? Clifton shrugs. "I'm used to it. I've heard people holler my name and nobody be in here," says the amiable woman who has been with the club for over twenty years. "It's just the way it is."

Indeed, this no-nonsense woman has multiple tales of strange, unexplainable occurrences while working at *The Longest Continuing Running Country Night Spot* in Cincinnati. Perhaps the most amazing aspect of it all, is the manner in which Clifton deals with things; she takes it all in stride. Moreover, she's even been known to give the ghosts a piece of her mind, if they're disrupting her work too much.

This sign is posted at the front door of Mackey's—at the insistence of Mackey's attorney.

"The water faucets used to come on by themselves and you'd go back to turn them off and turn around and they'd go right back on again. I'd just say 'stop this; I don't have time for this!'" says, Clifton, "and it quits."

This dark, dank landmark, located right across the river from Cincinnati in Wilder, Kentucky, has been visited by so many of the national psychics and ghost hunting groups that Clifton cannot even begin to remember them all, and they keep coming every year. Television crews from across the globe knock on Bobby's doors. Major networks, Sci-Fi Network, A & E, National Geographic Network, Discovery, StarZ, History Channel—pretty much you name it—they've been to Bobby Mackey's. They come to try and stir up the numerous ghosts that are believed to haunt the site for the ultimate paranormal glory: To capture them on film. They come because Bobby Mackey's is touted as the "Most Haunted Nightclub in America." Psychics are also drawn to the place in droves.

"The [ghosts] don't like psychics," says Clifton. "When a psychic walks through this door, you can always tell. They know it. They don't like pregnant women, either," the woman with a warm, quick smile and long dark braid adds.

Clifton, who offers haunted tours of the club, does not dispute that claim. Bobby Mackey himself, however, refuses to publicly admit that ghosts inhabit his joint. This, even though he wrote a ballad for Johanna, one of the resident spirits.

"Bobby says he doesn't believe there are ghosts there, but he won't be in the place by himself," Clifton notes. "I had to laugh at him. He said he came in one night and had a buddy with him, and he said he didn't turn any lights on and he was taking the money out of the machines. He said he looked up and saw these lights flashing. He looked down and the flashlight was going round and round. The flashlight fell and hit the floor and he just about jumped out of his skin he said, and he left."

Bobby Mackey's nightclub is filled with dusty remembrances from the past. Paintings of dancing Latin ladies frame the stage. They were hung years ago when another club (The Latin Quarter) was onsite, and yet they stay put on the walls. The tarnished bowling trophies from that era are found in the cluttered basement. To be sure, Bobby's is a country honky-tonk, with the finest of local music, including weekend gigs by Bobby Mackey and his Big Mac Band. Yet it feels undeniably eclectic—given its mish-mash décor and haunted reputation. Most everything that was there when Bobby bought the club in 1978 has stayed put, just like Bobby found them. He won't allow Clifton to change the décor, she says; he wants it just like it was. He doesn't even want things moved around from their original spots, either. Seems the resident ghosts have their own preferences about things at the club, as well.

"That one band that we had here, [the ghosts] didn't like them at all," says Clifton. That night, a regular customer, who also helps out at Bobby's, was sitting at the bar and "stuff started flying from the ceiling," says Clifton. "He looked up and there was nothing up there, but things were still hitting him in the face."

The band was very loud and very physically active. "They jumped all over the place," says Clifton, "and they don't like that so much." A few minutes after the ceiling incident, the same guy's cell phone started ringing.

"He asked me, 'Donna, where's the phone at?'" says Clifton, "and I said, 'it's on the hook,' and he said, 'Look. I'm getting a call from Bobby Mackey's and the phone's not even being used!' He ignored it," says Clifton, "but then a few minutes later *it* called back again and had 1-666-666-6666 all the way across it."

"He got three phone calls when that band was up playing," says the manager. The third time his phone rang, he quickly answered it, but it wouldn't let him connect. Instead, it went directly into his voicemail. "The voice said, 'Please, get them out!'" says Clifton. "Well he threw his phone across the room, and said, 'I'm done!'"

"He said it was a girl's voice, real scratchy. He saved the voice-mails and he let some of the ghost hunters hear them. I told him that he shouldn't give the ghost his phone number," Clifton quips with a wide smile.

Local writer Doug Hensley is the individual who brought the hauntings at Bobby's Mackey's to the forefront. Years ago, upon learning of the unexplained and frightening goings-on at this honky-tonk bar, Hensley knew it would make one heck of a nonfiction book. After several years of research and coaxing out first-hand interviews (and signed affidavits) from employees, bar patrons, and others, Hensley crafted a book that put Wilder, Kentucky and Bobby Mackey's on the map: *Hell's Gate: Terror at Bobby Mackey's Music World.*

Hensley noted that the original building on the Mackey's site was a slaughterhouse, erected in the 1850s. There is still a well in the basement of Bobby Mackey's where the blood and refuse of the slaughtered creatures was disposed of. Even though the slaughterhouse ceased production in the late 1800s, local legend claims that the basement was still put to use, as a secret site for occult rituals by satanic worshippers. It is widely believed that animals and maybe even humans, were sacrificed there.

The well, now sealed (mostly, it just won't stay filled to the top for some unknown reason), is a portion of the past that remains from the slaughterhouse structure. It is innocuous in appearance today, belying the disgusting and horrific happenings that have occurred there.

It is widely believed that part of southern Indiana socialite, Pearl Bryan, ended up in that basement well, but not while she was alive. Pearl was a southern Indiana beauty that fell for Scott Jackson, a dental student from a prominent family (who, unbeknownst to most, also happened to be an occultist). He seduced Pearl and she ended up pregnant.

Panicked, she turned to her cousin William Wood for help. Wood told Jackson, who arranged for Pearl to have an abortion in Cincinnati. Pearl was five months pregnant at this time and Jackson and his roommate, Alonzo Walling (a medical student) attempted the abortion. Despite multiple painful approaches including the use of cocaine and dental implements, they were unable to accomplish the deed and were likely left with a bloody, hysterical young pregnant woman.

The two calculating men then opted to do the unthinkable. They traveled back into northern Kentucky with an injured and suffering Pearl in tow. Then using the dental instruments they'd brought for the abortion procedure, they cleanly and precisely severed Pearl's head: From the coroner's report they did this while she was still alive. It is not known where she was murdered; some say it happened in the basement of Mackey's with her body moved and dumped by the river; others say it was the opposite with her head moved and dumped in the well.

Regardless, it is believed that Pearl Bryan now haunts Bobby's, searching for her head, which was never found.

The infamous well that has been on site since the place was a slaughterhouse. It was also the dumping place for animals, and perhaps even human remains, when the basement of the building was used for satanic practices many years ago.

The two murderous men were ultimately found out, and found guilty in a trial of epic proportions, and were the last two recipients of a public hanging in Campbell County, Kentucky. The men were offered life sentences in exchange for saying where Pearl's head was, but they refused (seemingly afraid of the wrath of Satan if they did so). It's also been written that numerous people involved with that trial were cursed with multiple instances of bad luck and dark ends. Scott and Walling are believed to be haunting Bobby Mackey's to this day, as well.

The slaughterhouse was ultimately razed, and a speakeasy and illegal gambling house was erected on the site. Murders were fairly commonplace there due to the clientele, and that the evidence (bodies) were usually dumped well away from the speakeasy to keep the cops at bay.

"Buck" Brady bought the club in the 1930s, and he turned the site into a popular casino and bar called the Primrose. Buck was harassed by the mob, however, which wanted to capitalize on his success, and even though he repeatedly refused, he ended up being ousted by their tactics, regardless. He eventually committed suicide. The ghost of Buck has also been seen at Bobby's.

The Latin Quarter nightclub was next to move in. Given its wicked and unlucky history perhaps contributing to the bad vibes, problems continued. Johanna, the club owner's daughter, fell for one of the singers at the club and became pregnant. "Daddy" didn't approve in the slightest and had the singer murdered. Johanna was livid and heartbroken. She first tried to poison her dad, and then committed suicide. Her lifeless body was found in the basement of the club. The coroner indicated that she appeared to be about five months pregnant. Coincidence?

In 1978, Bobby Mackey and his pregnant wife, Janet, impulsively bought the building, and Bobby began his mission to turn the site into a premiere and renowned country establishment.

Wasn't long, however, before the caretaker of the club, Carl Lawson, began seeing and hearing ghosts, and he ultimately ended up being possessed by them. Janet Mackey was harassed to the point of almost losing her and Bobby's unborn child (she was, like Johanna and Pearl, five months pregnant at the time).

From the moment they signed the purchase agreement, bizarre things took place. Waitress after waitress heard things, saw things, smelled things, and felt things. Lawson bore the worst of the paranormal brunt, however, and he underwent an exorcism in the 1990s. The unrest and frightening stories in the building continue on, despite this procedure, and probably always will.

"There was an exorcism done on Carl because he had the ghosts inside of him," says Clifton. "He still can't come back in today without things acting up. He doesn't come around much. You can just see the tension when he walks through that door."

The second to the last time Carl was in the club he saw Johanna on stage, standing behind Bobby, says Clifton, and he'd keep trying to go up and get to her on stage.

It's not only Lawson who sees the young woman, either. "I've had a lot of people ask me, 'who's that girl standing behind Bobby?'" says Clifton. Although she doesn't frighten easily, sometimes the ghosts at Bobby's get the best of her.

"When we used to be open on Thursday nights, I'd come in here to set the club up and put the chairs down," says Clifton. "I heard noises when I walked in the door, but you know, you learn to ignore them," she adds with a grin and a shrug. "Anyways, I was putting the chairs down and I dropped one. I heard this great big pounding behind here [the stage area/catwalk] and it didn't slack up. Just kept pounding. I ran that day. I didn't come back in until Bobby came down."

"The building's been there since the 1800s, and outside it probably looks like it's been here that long, too," Clifton says with a sly smile. She went on to say that a while back, Bobby had finally agreed that it was time to build a new club on an adjacent site and have the current building razed and used as a parking lot. However, an unknown force squelched those plans.

"When they got ready to pour the foundation, the ground cracked so they fixed it and were gonna redo it again—well, it cracked again," says Clifton. "Bobby gave up. He said 'somebody don't want me moving it.'"

The ghosts find unusual ways to let people in on their presence. "It's whatever they want to do," she says with a shrug. "I brought some people in here Tuesday night for a show and the ghosts started as soon as we walked in the door. There was beating on the walls and stuff like that. 'All right, we know you're here,'" Clifton says she told the ghosts out loud.

Before Clifton stepped foot inside Bobby Mackey's, she never even thought about ghosts. "The first time I got scared, I wasn't even working here then," Clifton says. "My ex-husband worked on the punching bag and the equipment for Bobby and there was a jukebox in here, and I brought his lunch down for him. I walked in the door and there was no music playing; nothing. I walked in the bull room and music immediately started playing," says Clifton, "and it was the Anniversary Waltz."

"I said, 'what are you playing?'" and my husband said, 'I'm not playing anything; it's unplugged.'"

Clifton shakes her head at the memory, still clear as a bell in her mind today. "That juke box was unplugged," she says, "and it was going around and around like it was playing a song on it—but the song it was playing wasn't even on the juke box! I left and swore I'd never come back here. A week later Bobby called me and asked me if I'd work for him," Clifton comments with a grin. Two decades later, she's still there.

Clifton does wonder if maybe the ghosts aren't trying to create havoc in the place at times. "I think the ghosts are the cause of some of the fights we have here," she says. "They [the ghosts] go around pulling hair, tapping people on the shoulder, doing strange things," she says, adding that it'd be easy to see how some of the club goers could assume that it's another patron, looking for a fight.

The unexplained incidents that happen on a regular basis at the club are astounding, at times.

"I had a guy that used to run the bull and he would talk to this ghost who had a long trench coat on, black cowboy hat, and a large, curled handlebar moustache," says Clifton. "He'd see the image of him there, standing by the end of the bar every day. It's only certain people that can see them," she adds.

Clifton has, herself, witnessed a full-bodied apparition. "Yeah, I've seen Johanna," she says. "It was a Thursday night [Clifton was prepping the club before opening]; Johanna was standing back in the corner. She had a long white dress on, long hair, and she was standing by the bull. Not doing anything. I wouldn't walk back there, but I knew it was Johanna."

Coates has seen Johanna "several times" and guesses that he's seen the ghost of Alonzo most often over the three years he's been with the club.

Clifton has also smelled roses—the scent that's attributed to Johanna. Many people over the years have smelled the telltale floral scent that Johanna imparts periodically at the site. She also advises pregnant women to avoid the club; given what's happened to Pearl, Johanna, and Janet.

"I had a group of people that I took around on Halloween," says Clifton. "I give a tour downstairs every year and there was one pregnant woman, and I told her that I wouldn't advise her to go in [downstairs]. She didn't listen to me; they got to the door and I went to turn the lights on, and none of the lights would go on. I couldn't do the tour without the lights on. As soon as the pregnant woman went back up the stairs, all the lights came on."

The ghost hunters have collected much evidence over the years, including a host of electronic voice phenomena. Clifton is the person that stays while the ghost hunting groups visit and she's also the only one who conducts the tours.

"I had two pictures taken downstairs on the stairway to no-where," says Clifton. "One group saw an image of a whole body on the steps."

Clifton believes that the spirits don't leave because Johanna said she would never leave here as long as her Robert Randall Mickey (Mackey) was here. "The guy that owned the club before was Robert Randall Mickey. The guy had the same scars that Bobby has."

One of the more incredible aspects of the hold this building has on Mackey is the inexplicable way he was drawn to it. "Bobby could tell you what this whole place looked like before he even bought it," says Clifton. "I think he's reincarnated. I asked Bobby, 'Do you believe in reincarnation?' Bobby said no, and I said, I think you are. It's so bizarre," she says, shaking her head. "There's no other way."

"I think that's what's drawing the people here," Clifton has told Bobby, but he won't admit he believes in ghosts. "People ask him that if he doesn't believe it's haunted, why doesn't he come in here by himself. And he says it's unexplainable," says Clifton. "He just can't explain it. I heard him tell one of his guitar pickers from the bluegrass show that this place was haunted, and I looked at him and he said, 'you didn't hear me say that!' Anybody asks

Bobby he'll say, 'I don't believe it.' His wife was even pushed down the steps when she was five months pregnant," adds Clifton. "She went into premature labor and almost lost the baby."

When asked if she'd give the author a tour of the basement, Clifton hesitated for a moment. "That is one place I don't like to go," she says. "Just as soon as I get down there, the hair stands up on my arms."

"You going down?" Coates asks her. Clifton cringes and nods slowly. "Sure you are," Coates coaxes with a smile. "It's not so bad in the daytime."

The basement is accessible only from the outside. You walk around the building to a separate entrance. People always want to see the infamous well and the stairway to nowhere. Even though you know it's called *the stairway to nowhere,* it's admittedly strange to see the wooden steps line right up to the ceiling and stop.

Old machinery and cast-off equipment are scattered throughout the vast cement cavern. There's what looks like an ancient casino table in the center of one room; its green felt, filthy and

torn to tatters. Cards and over-flowing ashtrays are resting atop the casino table, surrounded by three chairs. There are several empty beer bottles and some bar glasses scattered about. It was as if the tour had interrupted a ghostly game of Blackjack.

"There's no way I'll come down here myself," says Clifton. It's easy to see why.

The Stairway to Nowhere.

"I haven't been down here in this room with a tour in a while," Coates chimes in. "Last time we were down here with National Geographic and a little girl [ghost] was in the room/cell and throwing rocks at us." (Coates and Clifton played "roles" in reenactment for the National Geographic show.)

When asked to verify that there are children spirits on site, as well, Coate's nods grimly. "The reason the little girl's here was when the cult was in here, they believed that children who were mentally handicapped responded to the devil. So they locked them up in the jail cell over there, and sacrificed them back to the devil."

The cell is small, dark, and dank, brick from floor to ceiling. It's also where the mob would hide their alcohol during prohibition and lock it up with an alarm.

"There's actually two children here; one's a girl, one's a boy," Coates shares. "The boy was killed by one of the security guards from the Latin Quarter. He was killed on one of the back set of stairs. They threw him down the stairs. He busted his head and he died there. One of the captains of the door during the Latin Quarter told me that."

Down in the basement is also a back room that has what looks like faces on the walls, faces that just appeared from the rust and dampness. There is what looks like a goat and a woman with long hair and a hoofed arm. The basement feels creepy to be sure, but the whole building is game for paranormal visitors.

Most recently, something seems to have taken the stage. "The drums just start playing," says Clifton. Several employees have heard this and look to see that nobody is up there. "Those drums will play all the time. I'll tell Willie [Bobby's drummer] that somebody's been playing your drums," Clifton says. "You look up there and nobody's there. Things happen here and you can't explain it."

A local news station has been there three times, says Clifton, and each time their equipment blows up. They brought a generator outside last time and the generator wouldn't come on. They said they wouldn't come back, she shares with a smile.

According to Matt Coates, this is the jail cell in Mackey's basement where the Satanists kept the children for later use in their satanic rituals.

Margaret, who started witnessing at the bar a year after Bobby bought it has seen plenty, too. Margaret had no idea that the club might be haunted when she first started toting drinks.

"I guess the first thing I experienced was when I was putting out ashtrays, and I see this dog walking through the bar and I followed him but he disappeared. It was a large black dog, she says.

Macabre looking candles wait for an intimate dinner(?) in the basement of Mackey's.

"I wanted to know where he went! I didn't say anything because I thought they'd think I was nuts. I wasn't afraid, and I've had other things happen and I just figure it's normal… here."

Come to find out that Buck Brady had a large, black dog as his pet that was often on site with him at the Primrose.

"Things happen you can't explain, that's all I can really say," advises Margaret, who has been at Bobby's for close to thirty years. "There used to be this girl named Debby, and I was behind the bar, and I watched this man walk right behind her. He was tall. I said, 'Did you see that man?' Debby felt a man behind her, but there was no man there [he disappeared]."

Margaret recalls how the club "used to have a juke box and every time I'd go up to play it, somebody would whisper loudly, 'Margaret…' I quit playing it," she says. She's also often felt like people were behind her when nobody was there. "I've felt some-body touch me and look around and nobody was there. I've come in here a lot of times by myself and stayed for hours, and [it's been fine]," she says. "One time I was in the bar area [in the club alone] and heard people. It sounded like they were arguing. You could hear the girl cry. It was weird. It was really weird," Margaret admits. "And of course there was nobody back there," she adds. The long, curly-haired platinum blonde waitress, alone at the club, stayed strong, however, and didn't hightail it out the front door. Why?

"Well, I figured they'd settle it sooner or later," she replies matter-of-factly.

"You learn after a while," interjects Clifton. "Yeah, you know something might happen and if it does, you ignore them," adds Margaret. "A lot of times you're in the bathroom and the water starts running, and you're alone."

"Nobody would talk at first because we thought people would think we were [nuts]," says Clifton. Margaret nods in agreement. They started talking after author Doug Hensley compassionately coaxed the truth out of them. Finally, they were able to share what they'd experienced with each other. They are grateful to Hensley. Grateful, because now they can tell it like it is and not be afraid of what skeptics think.

Something is in the air at of Bobby Mackey's.

"There isn't anybody that can convince me that there ain't nothing here. I'm 100 percent positive there is," says Clifton. "They're here and they're not gonna leave."

Bobby Mackey's is located at 44 Licking Pike in Wilder, Kentucky. Web site: www.bobbymackey.com. Donna Clifton offers haunted tours of the club; check the web site for further information. Ghost hunters can book daytime and/or overnight investigations for a fee.

Who's got the beat? The drums have been known to play when Bobby Mackey and his Big Mac Band are away...

Chapter 35

A Visit with Renowned Cincinnati-Area Psychic and Clairvoyant, Victor Paruta

G hosts and psychics go together like Cincinnati and chili. So much so, it seemed like a fine idea to talk with local psychic Victor Paruta to pick his brain and get his specialized take on the tri-state haunted scene.

Q: How many years have you been working as a psychic?

I have been a professional psychic since 1990.

Q: When did you first recognize that you were psychic?

Although I did not consider myself psychic at the time, I started having vivid precognitive dreams at the age of fourteen or fifteen. I would have a dream and within a couple of weeks the dream would replay in real life, precisely as it happened in my dream. Although these dreams were simple moments from everyday life rather than predictions of significant events, they caused me to question the nature of reality.

When I was twenty, I had a spiritual awakening, which was brought about through practicing biofeedback. During this training one learns to control what were once thought to be autonomic physical activities such as heart rate and stress responses. It was as if a light came on inside and I felt oneness with everyone and everything.

A couple years later I joined a meditation group which was led by the most powerful psychic I'd ever me—Allain Ramsay. During our meetings, I experienced amazing psychic phenomena but still did not consider myself psychic. It was he who predicted that I would be doing readings. Although I did not believe him at the time, his prediction came true. Within a year and a half, I was doing card readings and my skills and popularity grew quickly. My clairvoyance really kicked in while studying with Ann Arbor psychic John Friedlander. My mediumship began when a close friend died and communicated with me, and through me to a friend, the evening of his memorial service. These experiences open psychic channels, which remain open once activated. I believe that everyone has the potential to be psychic. With curiosity and practice, these skills can be developed.

Q: What, in your opinion, are the most haunted local tri-state sites?

The tri-state has many well-known haunted buildings. I have personally experienced spirit activity in Bobby Mackey's Nightclub in Wilder, Kentucky, and had a client who became possessed there due to his own foolishness (he asked for it). He experienced a rapid series of tragic events, which ended after I cleared his energy field of entities. I have not personally investigated more than a couple of Cincinnati's most notorious haunted buildings. However, many of the most haunted buildings in the tri-state are not notorious or well known.

By far the most haunted building I'd ever experienced in Cincinnati is an old mansion near the Belvedere Condominiums on Reading Road in Avondale. The building was stripped of its once opulent interior features and converted to a nursing home in the 1970s. It now stands vacant and for sale, a mere shell of its former grandeur. I was showing it to a couple who were thinking of buying it (I occasionally work in real estate). I knew the second I laid eyes on the exterior that it was haunted. Once inside, I discovered that the building was full of very active ghosts who were trying to possess us. The male client did become possessed and had to be cleared after complaining of feeling sick and out of sorts.

Indian Hill, a very affluent section of Cincinnati, is very haunted. I have seen spirits walking the grounds of the stately homes located there. Haunted houses and locations are not at all rare. Ghosts are almost never malevolent. I have run into good-natured ghosts who remain attached to the homes they loved long after they died. I had a very pleasing interaction with one of these in an old farmhouse in the Milford area (northern Cincinnati). He had remained in the house after his death because of his fondness for the land and the life he had lived there. He was very aware of the current inhabitants and even interacted with them—this was verified during my interview with the current owners.

Q: What can "regular Joe's and Jane's" do, if anything, to increase their chances of encountering some paranormal phenomena while visiting some of the sites in the book? How can they avail themselves to it, but keep it safe?

It is important to surround oneself with protection before entering haunted locations. This is very simple to do. A short prayer asking for protection works very effectively. Surrounding oneself with a bubble of light or with angelic protection also works. You should not explore haunted locations when tired, sick, intoxicated or otherwise weak because you are more susceptible to possession when your energy is low. Your physical body is an excellent receptor of psychic energy. Be aware of cold or hot spots, goose bumps, shivers, and energy shifts as you explore. The five physical senses have psychic counterparts. You can hear and see with your mind in addition to your ears and eyes and this is usually how ghosts are heard and seen. I have seen ghosts with my physical eyes but when they sense that you can see them they usually disappear. Once I start looking for ghosts, my mind becomes more attuned to them and I start seeing them more easily and frequently. It's as if my mind starts refocusing itself so I can see them. An earnest and respectful attitude is best. Laughing and joking will prevent you from seeing.

Q: What are the most common types of hauntings?

The energies of a place can be from many and varied sources. There are usually layers of influences. First there are the earth energies—

*vortexes, ley lines, energy flows—often caused by the topography or un-
derground streams and caves. There are also imprints of all that has ever
occurred on the site, going back to prehistoric times. These imprints can
create energy patterns, which affect all that comes after. One often finds
that if there was a divorce or illness in a house, for example, subsequent
inhabitants are more likely to experience a divorce or illness. There are also
imprints of the people and events that have taken place there. Imprints
are more common than active hauntings. There are human ghosts, most
likely someone who has stayed in their house after they've died. Usually
they are afraid to move on into the spirit world or don't believe that one
exists. Their home is their safe place and refuge, so they stay. There are
also many denizens of the invisible realms including various nature
spirits—fairies, gnomes, etc.*

*During a psychic investigation, I always start paying attention to the
energies I am feeling on the land that the house is on. I also look at the
exterior of the house. What is the house communicating? If it says, "stay
out," then it is very likely haunted. I pay attention to the feelings I get
as I walk up to the door. Inside I walk around and sense the energies in
the house, usually starting with the first floor. I then do a walkthrough
of the entire house. The story of the house and its ghostly inhabitants
starts to reveal itself. Often, areas have very little energy and therefore
are clear. Sometimes there is a nonhuman presence, especially in base-
ments, from earth entities. Sometimes a house is part of a negative energy
web connecting several homes in an area. These can be held together by
negative entities. When the energy of one of these homes is successfully
cleared, then the entire web is weakened and everyone connected to the
web is relieved of the negative energy.*

I think it's fun to drive around and look at houses to see if they have a haunted vibe—they may seem to look back at you or their energy is more charged than the homes around them. There are itinerant ghosts who do not stay in the same place all the time. Some walk the earth or travel via vortexes.

Q: How can a person know if they are witnessing/ experiencing an imprint haunting versus an intelligent haunting?

Imprints do not interact with you. Ghosts can and do. Imprints are the echoes of the energies of the past. They will not notice you. Ghosts are "alive" so to speak. They may keep their distance or interact. With practice, a psychic can tell the difference between imprints and ghosts. Sometimes it's hard to tell.

Q: I've interviewed several people who've seen shadows/ dark faces/bodies. What does that typically indicate? Malevolent spirits or just simply a means of manifestation?

Good question! Best not to make hard and fast rules in ghost hunting. Each case should be investigated individually because shadows and dark-ness could be caused by a number of things. Sometimes imprints appear shadowy. One's mind can imagine things if they do not come fully into focus. I try not to rush to conclusions. It is okay to not be sure of what you are seeing for the moment and remain open minded. Shadowy or dark forms could be a means of manifestation or a means of perception by the perceiver. Most likely dark forms are not malevolent. Of course, the ghost could be that of a dark skinned person.

Q: In your years of experience, Victor, what have you found is the most common misconception people have about ghosts/psychics and the paranormal in general?

There are many misconceptions about ghosts, psychics, and the paranormal. Most misconceptions come from fear of the unknown. Most people do not think of ghosts as people, just like themselves, who have remained earthbound after death for a variety of reasons, some on purpose and some due to ignorance or fear. Ghosts do not haunt only graveyards or scary looking buildings. They can be found anywhere. Malicious ghosts are extremely rare, yet most people fear ghosts due to the scary stories they've heard around the campfires of their youth. If people were not as fearful of the dead or of their own mortality, their lives would be enriched.

Regarding psychics, some people place them on a pedestal, mistakenly believing that they are omniscient. Others believe the opposite—that all psychics are charlatans who trick people into believing they have special powers. The truth is that psychics are just regular people who have all the challenges everyone else has. Just as in any professional field, there are various specialties, skill levels, and ethical standards. Most psychics are genuinely interested in helping others. The abilities that psychics have are latent within everyone.

People tend to fear the world of the paranormal in real life, yet believe in Bible stories of paranormal events: angelic visitations, a virgin birth, healing the sick, raising the dead, turning water into wine, prophesizing, talking with the dead or with God, life after death, miraculous events. Even with so much paranormal activity in the Bible, many people find it difficult to reconcile their religious beliefs with the psychic side of life, as if the world of the Bible is not our world. In our world, most people are taught to believe that if you are talking with God and receiving answers, then you must be mentally ill.

Q: Do you receive any negative feedback in this day and age, about your profession? If so, does that surprise you?

I am fortunate to have a good reputation as a genuine psychic who is accurate and who conducts himself with a high level of integrity. Through my conventions and media work I have provided the community with many opportunities to explore the world of parapsychology. Personally, my study of metaphysics has provided me with a much deeper and more satisfying understanding of Life than traditional religious teachings. Because it worked for me, I believe it can work for others. I do not proselytize and also realize that this path is not for everyone.

It is important for psychics to know that they fulfill an important role in society and provide a service, which is needed. When one has a sense of purpose and value, one is no longer affected by the negative attitudes *of the ignorant. If the criticism is constructive, then one can learn from it. If it is not constructive, then it is important to stand strong and not allow someone's small mindedness to lower you.*

Q: Why do you think we have not quite jumped the hurdle in over-all acceptance of paranormal accounts/occurrences in our society? What do you think it will take for us to do so?

People are rightfully wary of being conned and manipulated. People have different ways of determining the truth of anything, including the truth of paranormal accounts, and usually the truth is difficult to determine. Various approaches have various limitations. The police, scientists, engineers use a very rational approach, collecting data and using logic. A lie detector may be used to determine if a suspect is lying. This approach can be successful but is limited by technology. For example, many people who have been convicted of crimes have been proven innocent after DNA technology was developed.

There is also the UFO phenomenon. There have been many personal accounts yet very little concrete evidence. Obviously there is something to the abduction experience. Yet it has been proven that eyewitness testimony is often inaccurate. Psychics use a more direct approach, bypassing laborious logical and evidence gathering processes and working directly with energetic imprints of what occurred. Of course, a psychic must have the insight and skills needed to retrieve accurate impressions that are not filtered through his own attitudes or memories. When psychics work with the police, they can provide clues which then direct the police to uncover evidence which was previously unknown to exist. Being skeptical yet open-minded is the best approach. If someone believes everything one hears then they are gullible and easily misled. If one is close-minded, one will not see the truth even when it is right in front of you. People are understandably wary of being manipulated and misled. Determining truth is a challenge and always will be because of our limitations. Talented psychics often transcend these limitations. Even so, there is a realm of Truth, which can never be proven and must be accepted as truth via faith.

Q: How many people would you guesstimate have contacted you over the years, seeking help/information about a haunted environment?

I have been a professional psychic for seventeen years and am contacted several times a year about ghosts and haunted places. Some hauntings are very simple to clear. Others are more complicated and require several visits. Now and then the negative energy of a place or person is impossible to clear. I am frequently asked to make contact with a deceased loved one.

Q: What stands out in your mind as the most incredible experience in your career so far? Was it appearing on national television? Helping an individual leave an evil entity behind?

Certainly being on The View was a highlight of my career. It was an exciting and very positive experience. However, when I think about the many mystical experiences I have had, the time the Virgin Mary manifested for a client during a reading would have to be one of the top experiences of my life. The unconditional love was so pure and powerful. We were both in awe. I will never forget what that felt like and the perspective on my life it provided.

There are many other peak experiences, some without simple explanations. A friend and I were walking in a park when we had a very powerful contact with an extremely large presence, which hovered over us. It felt like it was taking up the entire sky, horizon to horizon. It was a very humbling to experience such an enormous and awe-inspiring presence. It lasted for less than an hour. We couldn't explain it but both of us experienced it. Years later I read a very similar account on the internet written by a psychic whose experience took place on Glastonbury Tor, a sacred hill in England. She interpreted it as a contact with the Nordic ET's who are said to be very advanced and benevolent. When one is elevated in consciousness, the wonder, beauty and mystery of Life, which is always there, can be experienced and known.

Q: Can you expound a bit about your Victory of Light Festival (love the word play, by the way ;-) and your Mystical Tours?

The Victory of Light Psychic Festival was established in 1992 to showcase the world of the psychic sciences and intuitive arts. Many have called it one of the country's highest quality psychic fairs. It provides a venue for nationally and regionally known spiritual teachers, readers, healers and vendors. The festival is designed for the general public. I received the initial idea for the psychic festival from a psychic during a reading. Out of the blue she remarked that I should do a psychic fair. I liked the idea and started working on it. The first show was very well attended. The spiritual energy was high and kept building throughout the day. By early afternoon, a vortex started forming in the center of the room. An angelic being appeared in the vortex, its healing light flowing through the space in large, undulating waves. The space was filled with divine light.

Now, the Victory of Light Psychic Festival takes place at the Sharonville Convention Center the weekend before Thanksgiving and the first or second weekend in April. We are proud of the success and popularity of the two-day festival, which draws nationally known presenters and thousands of visitors, and has provided a quality venue for the region's most inspiring spiritual teachers, readers, vendors and healers.

Regarding Mystical Tours, I have always found travel to be a mind expanding experience and so started Mystical Tours to provide this experience to spiritually oriented, fun-loving travelers wishing to expand their horizons with others on the spiritual path. My favorite tour so far was to England and Ireland where we visited the great sacred sites of Stonehenge, Avebury Circle and Newgrange among many others. I was thrilled to find that the energy at these sites was very much alive and powerful. It will stay with me for the rest of my life.

Q: What is the most appealing aspect of being a well known and respected psychic and clairvoyant in the tri-state area?

As anyone else, I do enjoy being recognized occasionally. But my greatest satisfaction is when Spirit works through me to provide people with a level of guidance and healing which touches their souls. It is important to remember that it is not I but the Spirit, which moves through me, which allows a higher level of comfort and healing to take place. I'm happy when I'm able to step aside and allow this to happen. That is when my work is most satisfying.

Q: What is next on the horizon for you? Will you continue to teach psychic-awareness classes, for example?

I would like to continue to teach and to develop my shows. My dream is to write a book and, hopefully, I will do so in the next couple of years.

Q: How unusual (if at all) is it for a person (namely, me ;-) to trail along on her first investigation at a Middletown home and come away with multiple EVPs on her mini cassette recorder?

You are very fortunate to have discovered several good EVPs your first time out. Finding EVPs on tape requires many hours of very focused listening—and more patience than I have. I would agree that the place you recorded was very likely haunted.

Victor Paruta, Psychic, Clairvoyant can be reached at: Victor@ VictoryofLight.com. Phone: 513-929-0406, and web site: www. VictoryofLight.com.

Selected Bibliography

BOOKS AND PERIODICALS

Clark, Ryan. "Searching for Signs of Rebecca" October 31, 2006, *The Cincinnati Enquirer.*

Hensley, Doug. "Hell's Gate: Terror at Bobby Mackey's Music World," *Outskirts Press*, June 30, 2005.

McKibben, Paul. "Ghosts at Big Bone? Maybe," *Boone County Recorder*, October 26, 2006.

Rebecca McClung. Murder, *Miami Gazette*, 4-17-1901.

Spencer, Mark. "Oxford-Milford Road Motorcycle Ghost," *Hamilton Journal-News*, October 31, 1992.

—"Triple Axe Murders in Waynesville", *The Western Star Newspaper*, October, 1879.

—"Who Really Killed Rebecca Dawson McClung?" June, 1982 *Pulse-Journal*, Mason, Ohio.

WEB SITES

http://www.abandonedonline.net
http://www. americashauntedplaces.com

http://www.angelofthegarden.com
http://anomalyresponse.org
http://www.bobbymackey.com
http://www.canada.com
http://www.cityofmaysville.com
http://www.coax.net
http://www.darkfigureproductions.com/
http://www.enquirer.com
http://www.forgottenoh.com
http://www.graveaddiction.com
http://www.gregstorer.com
http://www.hammelhouseinn.com
http://www.invink.com
http://www.kypost.com
http://www.lovelandcastle.com
http://www.maysvillexplorer.com
http://www.maysvilleplayers.com
http://www.miamivalleyidol.com
http://www.ohioexploration.com
http://www.paranormalinvestigatorsofnky.com/
http://www.paranormalworlds.com
http://parks.ky.gov
http://www.prairieghosts.com
http://www.promonthouse.org
http://theshadowlands.net
http://www.southgatehouse.com
http://www.springgrove.org
http://www.strangehappenings.org
http://www.tearoses.net
http://www.the 20thcenturytheatre.com
http://uneasy_spirits.tripod.com
http://waynesgenhis.blogspot.com
http://www.yourghoststories.com

DVD'S

Dark Figure Productions, "True Ghost Stories from Ohio with Richard Crawford." 2006 DVD A documentary by filmmakers Andy Crosier and Richard Shane Reinert

Index

B

H

I

Indiana, 25, 211

Indian Hill, 227

Inglis, Mary, 184

J

Jackson, Scott, 211

Jefferson, Thomas, 184

Johanna (Ballad of), 209

Junie's Lounge, 134

K

KET/PBS, 71

Kinder, Jeff, 19-21

Kinder-Cross, Lisa, 19-21

Kings Mills, OH, 79-84

Kings Mills Technical Center, 80

Knights of the Golden Trail, 31-40

Q

S